E TAILL

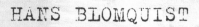

HANS BLOMQUIST

In Detail

with photography by Debi Treloar
and Hans Blomquist

RYLAND PETERS & SMALL
LONDON • NEW YORK

Designers Toni Kay and Lucy Gowans
Senior Commissioning Editor Annabel Morgan
Production Manager Patricia Harrington
Art Director Leslie Harrington
Editorial Director Julia Charles
Publisher Cindy Richards

First published in 2014 by
Ryland Peters & Small
20–21 Jockey's Fields,
London WC1R 4BW
and
519 Broadway, 5th Floor
New York, NY 10012

www.rylandpeters.com

10 9 8 7 6 5 4 3 2 1

Text © Hans Blomquist 2014
Design and photography
© Ryland Peters & Small 2014

ISBN 978 1 84975 551 1

A catalogue record for this book is available from
the British Library.

US Library of Congress cataloging-in-publication data
has been applied for.

Printed and bound in China

CONTENTS

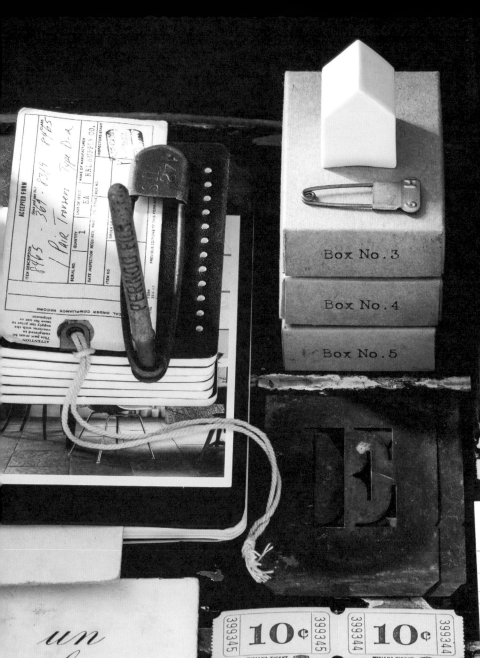

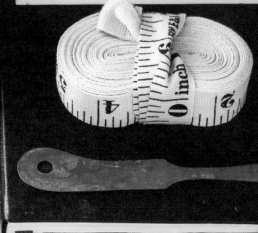

Introduction

I have focused on details ever since I got my first camera at the age of ten. I remember taking close-ups of surfaces, flowers, tree trunks, flaking paint, hands, faces, gravel and snow, as if my eyes didn't want to take in more than a small portion of the whole. Even now, as my partner likes to point out, it seems as if we've never actually been anywhere when we look through our holiday photos. There are just hundreds of details – windows, doors, colours, textures, plants, leaves, stones – and no one can tell where they were taken except me…luckily, I have a great memory for details!

Both at home and in my work as a stylist, getting the details right is key to achieving the perfect result. For me, the success of an entire room or photo can hinge on one seemingly insignificant element that makes the whole come to life. Some people like to look at the bigger picture first, but I am the opposite. I always start with a detail – a colour, a surface, a roll of string, a single flower. It could be anything, but from that single small piece of inspiration I will create a whole room set. I'm not a great fan of brainstorming meetings where concepts are endlessly discussed. Instead, I prefer to go for a walk and let the ideas start to germinate from the first seed of inspiration that plants itself. Then the rest – the strategies and all the other important aspects that need to be considered – flow on naturally from that.

In Detail illustrates the elements I think are so integral to a beautiful home, and explains how I use them as a starting point for creating a scheme. Natural objects and plants, interesting textures, colours you are drawn to, textiles that are pleasing to touch, and items that you love to collect and display are, collectively, what make a home welcoming and personal.

DETAILS

nature

favourite greens

Even though I love most trees and plants,
if I had to choose three favourites, it would
be quite easy (opposite). I have a soft spot for
fig trees – for the shape of their leaves and
their delicious fruits, but mostly for their
woody, aromatic scent. I love ferns in any
shape or form, and the fact that they can grow
almost anywhere makes them an easy choice
for the shadier areas of our garden. And last
but not least, I would choose olive trees, for
their silvery green leaves and their gnarled
trunks that have twisted into beautiful shapes.

natural wonder

We are lucky enough to have a lot of birds
that nest in the garden of our summer house
in the south of France. Last summer a couple
of birds made a nest in an old stone wall in the
garden, but the eggs were abandoned. I
checked every day for weeks to see whether
the birds would return, but when they didn't I
couldn't resist photographing the nest (this
page). Their smooth, tactile forms and the
blue-grey colour of the eggs were a wonder to
inspect up close, as was the marvellously
intricate form of the nest.

Nature is one of my greatest sources of inspiration. There are so many
amazing things to be found on a walk through a forest or field, or on a
beach. The colours and textures change every day of the year and there
is always something different every time I go exploring. Each season has
its own range of colours that is breathtakingly beautiful, from the pure
greens of the first leaves unfurling in spring to the fiery oranges and
yellows in autumn. I love seeing all the different textures, too, such as an
old tree trunk uniquely etched with the traces of time and weather. I
rarely try and force ideas to come, or look through magazines and blogs. I
prefer to go out for a long walk and just let my ideas develop. The silence,
fresh air and light open up my senses and give my thoughts free flow.

bulbs and tubers

One of the things guaranteed to put a smile on our faces after a long, dark winter is when the early spring bulbs and flowers start to appear in the florists' and flower markets. I can't resist buying an array of different bulbs to fill my home with flowers, as to me they bear the message that spring is just around the corner. I don't force bulbs to bloom early, although it is possible to do this by keeping them cool for a few weeks to simulate winter. Every bulb is different and some need more time than others, but normally it takes 8–15 weeks of being in a dark, cool place. Paperwhites (*Narcissus papyraceous*), which are a favourite of mine, don't need a simulated winter, whereas snowdrops require about 15 weeks. I think Mother Nature has her own way of doing things and we should not fool around with it – everything comes in time and we have to be patient enough to wait and enjoy it when the time is right. For the same reason, I would never buy strawberries in the winter, as they are an early summer fruit and the excitement of tasting the first of the year is so special.

under the snow

I come from a country that is covered with snow during the winter, and one of the first indications that spring is on the way is when the snow starts melting and the snowdrops appear. This sign of spring reminds me of my childhood, and now, living in Paris, I buy them every year, just so I can experience that same feeling that spring is not far away (opposite).

beautiful amaryllis

Amaryllis are one of my favourite bulbs. The flowers are so regal and beautiful, especially the very dark red ones, which look amazing atop their pale green stalks (below and below left). In Sweden, amaryllis are associated with Christmas, so even though I now live in Paris where you can buy them as early as October, I always wait until December – some traditions are so deeply rooted that it is hard to change them. Coincidentally, the name *Amaryllis belladonna* was coined in 1753 by the Swedish botanist Carl Linnaeus, who was born in Råshult, a village just a few kilometres from my hometown.

Every season has its own range of colours that is breathtakingly beautiful, and the fresh pale green of spring's optimistic first shoots is particularly inspiring and uplifting for the soul.

jardin

ready to grow

There is something very beautiful about the texture and colour of bulbs – and their ability to produce flowers is one of nature's miracles. These bulbs are paperwhites, and I don't think you can ever have too many around the house, as the scent of their multi-layered flowers is amazing. I always buy them as soon as they come into the flower shops, so I can plant them and watch them grow from day to day. I keep them in a dark, cool place until they have grown quite large, then I often display them in clear glass bulb vases – I find their roots intriguing.

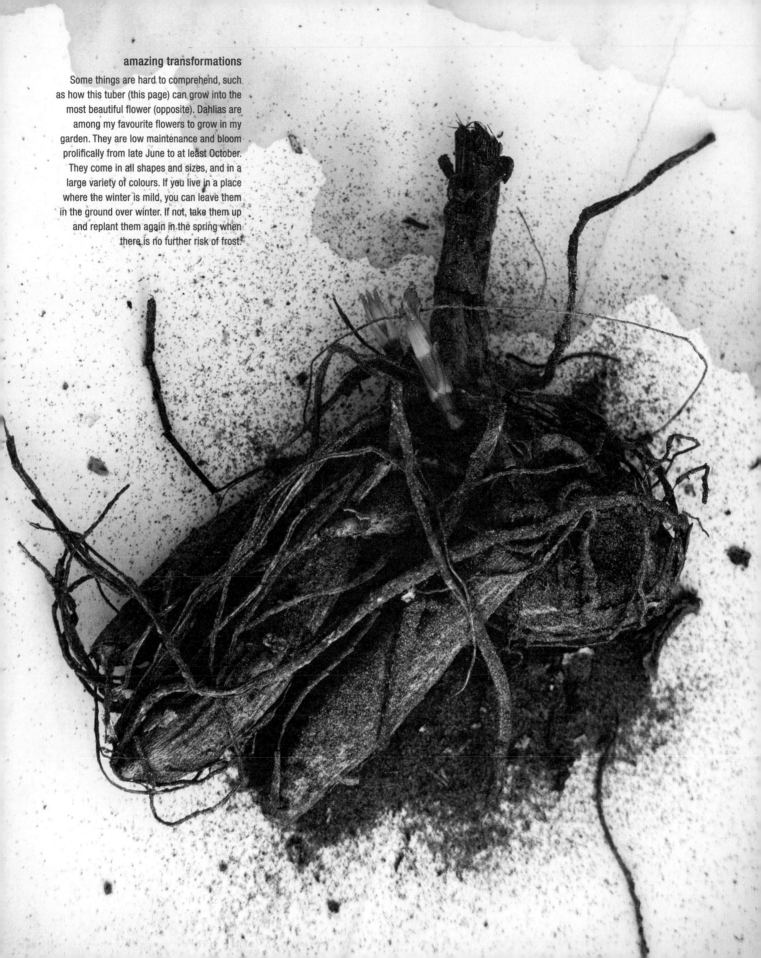

amazing transformations

Some things are hard to comprehend, such as how this tuber (this page) can grow into the most beautiful flower (opposite). Dahlias are among my favourite flowers to grow in my garden. They are low maintenance and bloom prolifically from late June to at least October. They come in all shapes and sizes, and in a large variety of colours. If you live in a place where the winter is mild, you can leave them in the ground over winter. If not, take them up and replant them again in the spring when there is no further risk of frost.

pretty spring

One of the things I love to do in early spring is to walk around Paris and look at all the cherry trees laden with blossom. Of course, I feel tempted to break off a large branch, but how could I? Everyone should be able to enjoy these beautiful trees, so I buy branches of blossom to display at home. Sometimes I try to tell a little story by creating a still life to suit the type of flowers I have brought home. Here, I created a romantic setting for the delicate pink flowers (opposite). Magnolias (right) are another spring favourite that are as beautiful inside as out. I added a nearly black hand-painted backdrop to bring out the deep pink of the petals.

prop flowers [overleaf]

Some of the photoshoots I work on require a lot of flowers, especially if the theme is romantic or decadent. I love doing these shoots, mostly because I really enjoy creating oversized bouquets (page 21). There is something very rewarding about mixing and matching so many different shapes and colours of flowers to produce a very personal and special effect. It reminds me of the stunning large floral displays that were created in castles and grand houses in the olden days. The extra bonus is, of course, that if these shoots take place in Paris, I can bring the flowers home and recreate a similar arrangement to enjoy.

blossoms and flowers

There are few things that add as much colour and happiness to a home as flowers – aside from family and friends, of course. I try to bring flowers into my home every week, as it makes such a difference to the way I feel and injects a sense of vitality that only flowers can achieve. Cut flowers can be expensive, but there are so many flowers growing in abundance in the garden and on common land that can make an even more beautiful bouquet than shop-bought flowers would do. Just make sure that you pick only common wildflowers and foliage from large patches where the growth is abundant, and always pick in moderation without damaging the roots. I am lucky enough to often be able to take flowers home from photoshoots that I have worked on where they have been used as props, but I also try to get out of Paris from time to time to pick some freely growing spring or summer flowers, as they are what I really prefer. The changing seasons mean that you can create different arrangements throughout the year.

STEM of
Vitis Hookeri, M. Law.
KHASIA.
SIR J. D. HOOKER

1878

PULVIS

I don't have a preferred season when it comes to flowers, as there is always something amazing to be found, whether in the florists' or growing naturally. It is nice if one can create different kinds of arrangement and vary the flowers you choose. In Paris I have discovered some amazing flower shops, where the owners are very creative and the choice of flowers they offer is so different and unusual. There are no standard cultivated cut flowers for sale in these shops; the selection is wilder and more interesting, and more closely reflects what you find growing naturally. That is exactly what I look for, as I don't much care for the forced cut flowers that you find everywhere. I wish more florists would be daring in sourcing their stock, so more of us can enjoy the true beauty of the amazing blossoms and flowers that nature produces. Remember, too, that you don't need to compose a large, full bouquet to create impact. Sometimes a single stem or branch of blossom can be just as striking and effective as a more generous display.

more favourites

When it comes to flowers, there are a few that I enjoy more than others, such as poppies in any shape or form, especially the wild ones that grow in fields and along country roads in early spring, with their thin paper-like petals that move softly in the wind. Poppies (opposite) are extraordinary both for the shape of their buds before they open and their range of vibrant colours. Their stems bend and grow in any direction, so it is easy to create a stunning display in a simple vase. Fritillaries (above right) are another favourite, as I find the patterned petals so beautiful and intriguing – another exquisite product of nature for us to enjoy.

left to dry [overleaf]

Anyone who follows me on Instagram knows that I find dried flowers, such as these roses, dahlias and tulips (right and pages 24 and 25), so striking. There is something about the colours of the petals when they have dried to an almost antique or vintage shade that I find so beautiful. I always leave flowers in their vase long after their 'best-before date' has passed, and I think they are just as lovely as on the day I bought them, if not more so. Make sure you pour the water away, though, as otherwise it will become smelly.

play with scale

When displaying a large branch in your home, you don't have to use a large vase. I like to play around and create settings that are not perfect or by the book. I found that this vintage glass bottle worked really well as a vase for the oversized branch, making it look a bit different. The vase doesn't detract from the beautiful white blossom branch, but holds it in place effectively, and the two pieces work in harmony to create a distinctive display.

PARAFFINUM LIQUIDUM B.P.

boughs and branches

No matter what time of year it is, nature always provides something that will create a beautiful focal point in any room, and bring a little piece of the natural world to your home.

There is so much beauty in nature that can be brought home to make a striking arrangement on a table or sideboard. I nearly always come home from my walks in the forest bearing a large branch with either green or dried leaves, as both look stunning in any setting. Even when the leaves have dried out, the branches still look elegantly sculptural and can be enjoyed for a long time. I look out for different dried bushes and small plants, too, as their twisted, wiry shapes make stunning additions to any display. Such twigs and branches can also be propped up on their own on a side table to create a beautiful focal point and add a piece of nature to any room.

free forms

One of the best things about finding branches and boughs to display at home is that they are free, and I prefer them to anything I could buy from a florist because they can be used to create much more personal and interesting arrangements. Tall grasses, dried out and wiry in texture (below left), or a dead branch from a bush, twisted and sculptural (below right), will make a more striking natural addition to your home than a perfectly bound bouquet. Add some favourite complementary objects to your setting to create a still life.

multi-use

When bringing a large branch into your home, you can simply lean it against a wall or put it in a vase, or you can make it into something useful, such as a new lamp, as I have here (opposite). Wrap the long cord around a couple of the branches so that you are sure it is secure and add a decorative light bulb to create an unusual and cosy corner.

a little bit of forest

I think that every home needs something living in it to add an extra layer that makes it soft and welcoming. A large, leafy branch brings a little bit of nature into the home and is a good alternative to a pot plant (this page). The old British bus numbers hanging on the wall behind form a graphic vertical runner and an effective foil for the natural element. I discovered the bus numbers in an antiques shop in Los Angeles, so they had travelled a long way from home!

In my opinion, you can't go wrong when bringing any kind of branch, stick or dried grasses into your home as a natural decoration for any setting, and the fact that they will last almost forever is a bonus. In winter, I love to bring in bare branches, large or small, and in spring and summer it is either branches laden with blossom or lush green leaves. One of my favourites are, of course, olive branches, which still look so beautiful when they have dried out. In autumn, there are many different kinds of berries that look striking and add a splash of colour.

autumn beauties

Even though I don't really like it when summer starts fading into autumn, the days get shorter and I know there is a long winter ahead of us, I do love it when berries of any kind start to appear. Among my favourites are blackberries (left) and rose hips (opposite). We always pick blackberries in early autumn at my house in the south of France to make jam, and I always bring home some branches for display. Later in the year, vivid red rose hips make great Christmas decorations. They last a long time without water, so here I placed them in a large wire basket to create a different setting.

STOP TALKING

bundle of joy

I found this bundle of *Diplocyclos palmatus* (this page), an ornamental vine native to rainforests and commonly known as native bryony or striped cucumber, in a flower shop in Paris and thought it was the most beautiful thing I had seen in a long while. The green and orange fruits with uneven white stripes, hanging on dried, wiry, string-like stems, would add interest to any kind of display. I placed them with a selection of flea-market finds gathered over the years. The Slaymaker Lock Company sign (opposite) was purchased in New York City – in addition to manufacturing locks, the firm also produced house numbers and these letters. The cone-shaped cardboard bobbins were originally used for thread and string.

natural display

A simple bunch of bare branches in a
large, coloured glass vessel adds texture
to this living room (this page). The room
has a spontaneous and natural feel, both
in the mixture of materials and textures,
and in the way it is furnished (opposite).
I love entering and spending time in rooms
that look as though they have just come
together without being too well planned.
It makes me feel very relaxed and at home.

plants and pots

Readers of my first book, *The Natural Home*, will know that I believe plants are one of the most important additions to any room. To me, a home without these green wonders feels slightly boring and devoid of life. I have many plants at home, even though it is quite hard to keep them alive, as I travel frequently for work and can't always find someone to come in and water them. If I can, I take them with me when I go on holiday, but some of them have now grown far too large to fit in the car. These I give bottles of water that last for two to three weeks, so there is a better chance that they will be happy and thriving on my return. I am always upset when a plant doesn't survive, as they are such a part of my life at home. Even though I immediately replace them, it takes time to get them into the same welcoming shape.

no plastic

When I am planting at home, I use pots made from natural materials, such as bark or terracotta (below left and right). I also make my own pots from old newspapers for growing cuttings or smaller plants, as when they are ready to be planted you can simply place them straight into the ground or a larger pot complete with the paper (opposite). I never use plastic containers because there is nothing you can use them for afterwards. For this reason, I always remove plastic pots from the plants I buy in a nursery or garden centre. I don't want to bring them home just to throw them away, and in that way the nursery can use them again for new cuttings and plants.

Plants add a very special atmosphere to any home and help bring it to life. They grow so well into the space that they become an integral part of the whole décor.

everything works

If you don't have green fingers or much success with houseplants, you can always bring home a large branch of leaves and berries, which will, for a while, give you the same effect (this page). Place it in a spot where it will take centre stage, so you can enjoy it to the full. I love to have both branches and plants in my home. This lush green fern is planted in a square, weathered zinc pot, which makes an eye-catching combination (opposite).

Scented geraniums are so easy to grow and fill
the home with an uplifting fresh fragrance.

scented favourites

I absolutely love scented geraniums. I have a few at home and can't really
choose a favourite among them, as they are all equally heavenly. They grow
very easily and last well over winter if you bring them inside and give them
less water, then cut them down (this page) and replant them in spring to get a
healthier plant that grows well and full over the summer (opposite).

texture

tactile still life

Adding texture to your living space doesn't require large pieces of furniture or peeling walls. A rustic antique wooden chair in front of an old paint-spattered cloth can do the trick (opposite). Add a few carefully chosen objects, such as a coil of rope, a ball of string and some pieces of fabric, for a layered effect.

some favourites

Collected here are some of my all-time favourite props that I use to add extra texture when I am styling an interior for a photoshoot (this page). I have gathered a number of such items over the years, mainly from different flea markets around the world, and they have been so useful for adding that extra touch of visual interest that is needed in pictures.

Texture adds an extra dimension to any interior. It creates both depth and a layered effect, which enhances the feeling of a three-dimensional setting and gives the space life. I add a lot of texture to my interiors, first layering different materials, such as wood, metal, stone and concrete, to create a foundation, and then building up the picture by using textiles in a mix of fabric types, weaves and colours. In newly built homes or very modern settings, adding a combination of textiles and some vintage pieces of furniture or accessories softens the space and creates an inviting atmosphere. Conversely, houses or apartments that already have a lot of texture in both the walls and floors can be helped by bringing in sleek contemporary furniture and objects for contrast. Texture is one of the most important ingredients for creating a successful interior, and I always find that mixing old with new and rough with smooth creates a home that is both interesting and personal.

wood and metal

I am a big fan of all natural materials, but wood and metal must be my favourites. I also love leather, stone and concrete, as they have the same quality as wood and metal in that they age well, both due to everyday wear and tear and from the passing of time. All these materials become more and more beautiful the more they are used. In the same way that an old leather jacket or a pair of jeans grow softer and more comfortable the more they are worn, furniture and objects made from these natural materials take on a rich patina through age and use. I am not suggesting that you should deliberately distress anything to make it look old and worn – it is a process that will happen naturally through daily use. It is important to take care of your furniture and other pieces but don't be too precious about it – these items are there to be used and enjoyed every day.

wooden mix

The mix of different woods in this kitchen of a loft in Brooklyn, New York City, is really cleverly done (opposite). The greyish tone of the cupboard doors, the untreated wood of the tabletop and the bench made from recycled wood work so well together. The black-painted wall and concrete floor provide the perfect backdrop to tie all the elements together. The plant and herbs introduce a green accent and the addition of the draped tablecloth softens the space.

smooth storage

These zinc trays have a very smooth, matt finish from years of use (right). Lined up on a kitchen counter, they provide easily accessible storage for vegetables, knives and forks, or other frequently used cooking utensils. The knife holder in the background was made by cutting a long, narrow hole in the work surface. The knives slot in easily and are always within reach.

stripped bare

Everything about this setting is both beautiful and inspirational. First and foremost, the space itself is exceptional, with large factory-style windows, a high ceiling and the smooth concrete floor. And then there's the way the furniture has been placed in the middle in a simple but inviting setting. I love the deconstructed sofa and armchairs, as you can see the construction, the worked vintage wood, the springs and the original calico lining. I know this may not be everyone's cup of tea, but to me it is perfect.

I never buy materials that have a very fragile surface, as it is so irritating when the first scratch appears – and this is always more visible on a shiny finish. I prefer materials such as wood and metal to have a raw, unpainted finish, as untreated wood gets better and better the more it is used and the character of the metal also changes over time. Zinc is one such metal that I love, as the surface becomes very smooth and matt with use, which to me looks so much nicer than when it is shiny and new. These natural materials also work well in combination with one another, the soft quality of wood balancing the harder metal. I also mix untreated wood with vintage and weathered wood, as they complement each other beautifully.

in the mood for wood [previous spread]

The previous spread shows my work space at our summer house in France, where I love to sit and work or just daydream (page 49). I have gathered some of my favourite wooden items and put them on display on both the wall and work surface. The desk was made from an old door found at a flea market, and is supported by antique wooden trestles. It fits into the space perfectly and ties in beautifully with the dark, matt painted wall. The stool was bought at the same time – and how could I resist it, as a painter somewhere in France had used the seat as his paint palette. The vintage bobbin stand (page 48) is perfect for holding bills, letters and other things that need to be remembered.

out in the open

In some areas in a home, such as the kitchen, open storage works particularly well (opposite). It not only makes it easy to find everything quickly, both when preparing food and setting the table, but it also makes a nice display area, where you can showcase all the things you love, from salad bowls and platters to stacks of plates and glassware. It is also the perfect home for cookbooks, so you don't have to run to a bookcase elsewhere every time you want culinary inspiration. These raw metal shelves give a contemporary utilitarian look, reminiscent of a restaurant kitchen, which I have always found appealing.

textural treasures

Vintage wooden clothes pegs (above right) are both useful and attractive to incorporate into a display. Use them for drying clothes, of course, but also to display posters instead of picture frames. The solid metal fishing weight (right) has a pleasing vintage texture that works really well with the faded string.

mix and match

A bold combination of different materials creates
a very personal, textural setting. It is always intriguing
to see how several materials mixed together can create
a completely different look from when only one or two
are used. The tiled wall (opposite) creates an unusual
backdrop for a dining space and works especially well
with the different wood finishes, the shiny metal of the
table leg and the blend of colours, resulting in a setting
that is contemporary and interesting. The textiles and
fur bring texture and warmth to the space, while the
plants add life and a touch of nature. The sleek finish
of the wooden sideboard shown on this page is offset
by the large twisted branch.

When you buy vintage or antique furniture, I think it is important to resist the temptation to sand it down or repaint it. Changing it in any way will alter the character of the entire piece and devalue it. The beauty of antique furniture is that it bears the traces of time and a long life, and in most cases the unique patina is so beautiful that it should be cherished and admired. When such pieces are altered, the danger is that they will simply look like cheap versions of what they once were. And once the texture is modified or the colour is scraped off, there is no going back to the original finish. To me, there is nothing more beautiful than an old piece of furniture that is still intact and is reminiscent of the era and time when it was made.

wooden inspiration

The dominant material in my work space in our flat in Paris is wood. I found the wooden trestles abandoned on the street and added a top to make a small desk that fits perfectly between the windows (opposite). The worktop is covered in an artist's canvas that I painted a pale sand colour. This is a great solution if you want a surface that you don't have to be too careful with, and it is easy to re-cover if you want to change the look.

a passion for texture

One of my favourite things in our apartment in Paris is the wooden floor, which is original and dates from 1850 (below left). It is so full of texture and character. Vintage rope is something I always have close to hand, because it is both useful and beautiful to look at (below right).

Metal is often considered to be hard and edgy, but it is easy to soften it up by combining it with textiles and other natural materials such as wood, leather and concrete – all of which become more beautiful with age and use.

Nature is a treasure trove of inspiring finds, from dried leaves, flowers and twigs to many other pleasing objects. Whether it's the shape or colour that you find appealing, they can be used to add textural interest to any display or still life.

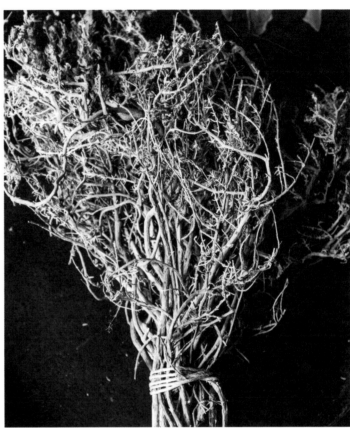

dried and textural inspirations

built with love

These dried inspirations were gathered on walks in the south of France. The wild thyme (above right) is delicious to use in cooking. The bird's nest (opposite), so carefully built, is like a piece of art. The abandoned quails' eggs are also exquisite objects that can only be admired for their beauty.

uncovered [overleaf]

I love these characterful old armchairs (page 58) for their shape, style and layers of texture. The bunch of dried corn on the cob, found at a flower market in New York City, has great textural beauty.

Nature is my greatest source for dried and textural finds that make wonderful additions to any interior. Whether interesting for their shape or colour, they work well in any display or still life, either adding to the textural mix or acting as a foil for objects with a glossy or polished finish. I don't think I have ever come home from a country walk empty-handed. Most of the time, my prize is something dried, with a shape or texture that I love, or some flowers, stones or pieces of wood. In the south of France I sometimes gather the wild thyme that grows everywhere – it looks beautiful, the scent is heavenly and it is tasty in cooking. I would never take a bird's nest from a tree, but I can't resist ones that have fallen to the ground. I am so amazed by the work that the birds have put into them – searching for pieces of grass or twigs and branches, and, with only their beaks for tools, building the most beautiful home for their eggs. It's a true act of love.

peeling paint and surfaces

Textured walls, with patches of bare plaster showing through layers of peeling paint and faded wallpapers, will add depth and interest to any style of interior. The eye-catching backdrop is such that, even if you furnish the room in a very sparse and contemporary style, it will still look warm and welcoming. Alternatively, you can embrace the vibe wholeheartedly and add even more layers of texture via your choice of furniture and objects. There is something about highly textured walls that I find really beautiful. Being able to see, in places, the many different layers and colours of paint and wallpaper that have been added throughout the years is intriguing. It is fascinating to trace the various interior trends that have been and gone, just by seeing what style of wallpapers were used during which periods.

on reflection

Create depth in a room and increase the sense of space by hanging an oversized mirror on one wall (opposite). As well as making a room feel larger, it will help to maximize the natural light coming in through the windows by bouncing it around the room. A mirror also adds texture, as everything is reflected and multiplied. Here, the peeling paint and paper on the wall above the mirror has been left for its textural appeal. The different woods of the table and chairs contribute to the scene and add a softer element to the mirrored setting.

peeled and revealed

The layers of texture on these walls (above and left) have been created by scraping or rubbing off old paint to reveal the previous layer – or layers – beneath. The brass wall lamp adds another surface and contrasting texture to this setting (above left), and makes it feel a little more polished.

looking back

This house in the south of Sweden has not been renovated for many years. To me, it is exquisitely beautiful, both in terms of the colours and textures and also because you can see how the walls were painted and decorated at the time when the house was built. The house is furnished with simple furniture, including garden chairs and vintage fruit crates. Even though it is quite a mishmash, it all works perfectly together.

layered textures

This loft apartment in New York City (left) has many different layers of texture. The distressed walls are the backdrop to the rest of the materials used in the kitchen area, which include raw metal worktops that are prevented from looking cold or hard by the juxtaposition of the untreated wood cupboard doors. The wall lamps have been cleverly integrated so that no flexes can be seen.

moody

This work space is in the same beautiful house in Sweden that is shown on the previous spread (opposite). Here again, there is real treasure for a texture lover. The peeling wall mixed with the used and worn wooden furniture results in a space that is a joy to be in. I added the branch hanging in the window, as I felt something organic from nature was missing when we took this picture.

Adding a textured effect to the surface of a wall can be quite tricky, as if it is not extremely well executed it will look fake and flat. If your heart is set on textural walls, do some research beforehand to ensure that you will be happy with the end result. A failsafe alternative is to choose an interesting paint colour and brush it on loosely and messily to create a scuffed, mottled effect.

I would love to have peeling, textured walls at home, but everywhere I have lived to date has been stripped bare by a previous owner. One day, I hope I will live in a beautiful space where the original walls and floors have been left intact and where you can see the traces of passing time. Such places are increasingly hard to find, as most have been re-done in one way or another, but I hope that someone has saved some textural treasures for me to discover.

peeling paint

I found these small folding chairs in a junk shop in the south of France close to
our summer house and immediately fell in love with the peeling paint and the
beautiful hue of the wood showing through in places (opposite). The owner of the
shop suggested that they might once have been used around a swimming pool.
I don't know if that is true or not, but I do know that I wouldn't dare to relax and
lean back on one, as it would most likely collapse.

textural wallcoverings

If you are not fortunate enough to have inherited walls that are already textured through years of use, you can cheat and create your own. Whether at home or at work as a stylist, I like to be able to change a room in an instant without going to too much trouble, so I am always dreaming up unusual ideas that are easy but effective. Giving a wall a textured finish is quick and simple – whenever you feel like experimenting with a different texture or colour, choose any kind of paper or fabric and attach it to your walls using masking tape or adhesive putty.

botanical beauty

I love pressed flowers, especially vintage ones with evocative old labels on yellowed paper. These ones were bought in Sweden and given to me by a stylist friend (opposite). I stuck them up with adhesive putty, commonly known as Blu-Tack or Poster Putty, on an otherwise white wall in our summer house, and the display instantly made a huge difference to the entire room.

yesterday's papers

As I am a fan of typography and especially vintage newspapers, nothing could make a better wallcovering than these old French newspapers, some of which are more than 100 years old but still intact, and with a very beautiful texture that makes someone like me very happy (right). For a multi-layered, textured wall, simply attach each sheet individually using adhesive putty. To achieve a cleaner, flatter finish, first tape the sheets of paper together on the back and then fix these larger sheets up on the wall. The choice is yours, but either method will result in a beautiful textural wall.

soft and welcoming

Upholstered furniture or different types of seating made of any material – as long as it has an interesting finish, character or shape – are great ways of introducing additional textures to a living room. You can mix and match pieces, trying out different types of furniture until you achieve the look you are after. I like to play around with texture and colour using a balance of different materials – textiles with different weaves, both fine and coarse, and a combination of materials with disparate qualities, such as wood, metal and rattan. It can also be interesting to put together seating of different styles using a mix of antique, vintage and new.

centre stage

There is a wonderful and unusual mixture of textures in this living space (left and opposite), in which a vibrant green sofa takes centre stage. I particularly love the screen that separates one part of the room from another. Made from old doors, it creates a striking backdrop that holds the whole setting together in such an interesting way. Its rustic quality also accentuates the streamlined shape of the sofa, making it look modern and slick by contrast, even though it is actually a vintage piece. In addition, the combination of different textiles, wood and rattan gives a soft and welcoming feel.

please be seated

I love everything about this apartment near Union Square in New York City. The exposed brickwork, the beautiful hue of the wooden window frames with the remains of paint still visible in places, and the smooth, well-worn wooden floors all create a beautiful and unobtrusive backdrop. The mix of furniture, where soft vintage shapes meet more industrial pieces, and the different shades and subtle patterns of the upholstery make the whole setting feel soft and welcoming.

colour

creative spaces

I have always had a soft spot for artists' studios – the concentration of colour and creativity is so inspiring. I experiment with colour a lot – it's important to constantly explore and discover fresh colour combinations for my styling work (opposite).

personal favourites

At home, I opt for a muted colour scheme, ranging from calm neutrals to dark, thundery greys. I also love soft pastels, as they complement both lighter and darker shades. I store my paint samples in glass jars (below); each one is labelled with its NCS (Natural Colour System) code, so I know I will pick exactly the right shade when decorating.

Colour is such a personal thing. Some of us have a passion for pale, faded hues, others gravitate towards moody tones. Vibrant primaries might be your thing, or the bold contrast of black and white. There is no right or wrong when it comes to colour – the most important thing is choosing a scheme that you love. As you will be able to tell just from glancing at this book, my preference is for a colour scheme that is muted, soft and atmospheric, and I almost always draw inspiration from nature. The rich brown of an autumn leaf might inspire me to paint my bedroom wall exactly the same shade, or the ominous grey of storm clouds may suggest the perfect colour for a sofa or other textiles. There are a million possibilities when it comes to the colours of the natural world.

dusty pastels

Pastels have a soothing, feminine effect. They combine well with other colours, both darker and lighter, and they work effectively either as a backdrop or as an accent colour. You can team them with thunder grey, muddy brown or indigo blue for a sophisticated effect, or with white or lighter shades for a soft, warm feel. My personal favourites are dusty pink, smoky grey, duck egg blue and faded, vintage yellow, but to prevent them from looking too sugary or twee, I look for slightly 'dirty' shades that contain minute traces of black pigment – this is what gives these colours the aged, subtle effect that I love.

When it comes to finding the right pastel shade, there are so many different paint brands and colours to select from that the choice can seem overwhelming. Look at a few different ones before you make your final decision, as paints vary greatly in colour, finish and quality. I prefer to use paint that is environmentally friendly and I nearly always choose a matt finish – I like the subtle, slightly textured effect. I also tend to use more expensive paint because it usually provides better coverage, which means your walls will require fewer coats. And I am always drawn to paint brands with a large selection of muted, natural hues.

rough and ready

Apart from painting the walls, the quickest and easiest way to inject colour into your home is to use textiles. This upholstered sofa (opposite) had been stripped back to its bare bones, and I covered it with a thick canvas that I painted myself. So easy and simple, but it works.

relaxed rose

Faded rose pink has a subtle, undemanding quality that means it works well in any interior. Prevent it from looking too sugary-sweet by taking inspiration from nature and pairing it with a vivid green hue like these underripe blackberries (below left) or even with glossy black, as with these vintage labels (below).

dusty answer

Mix faded pastels and you will get an elegant and understated interior. In this dining area (this page), warm stone grey walls are enlivened by a vintage shell pink lampshade hung from a length of rope. The pale, untreated wood of the chairs and table brings texture, while the black bucket creates contrast and adds depth. The space has all the calmness and serenity of a Dutch still life.

back to nature

Lupins (opposite) are a particular favourite of mine – they remind me of childhood summers in Sweden, where they grow lavishly along every roadside. These varieties contain many beautiful hues of dusty pink and purple – the perfect inspiration for a pastel scheme.

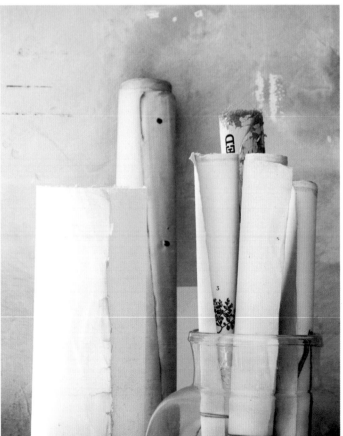

light and bright

Colours can vary greatly depending on the environment, which is why so many people opt for plain white walls – it's a safe bet, and you know you won't have any horrible surprises when the decorating is finished. White is classic and timeless. It provides a clean, simple foil for most other colours, and it makes a room feel fresh and bright, even on a dark and dreary day.

At home in Paris, my living room is painted white and I sometimes think that perhaps it was a bit of a boring choice – the safe option. From time to time, I wish I had been more adventurous. But white just seemed like the right choice at the time and every springtime, when the room is flooded with dazzling sunlight after a long, dreary winter, I remember how much I love my white walls.

White does tend to change with the light, so you will have to experiment to find exactly the right shade to suit your home. Luckily, paint manufacturers have created a huge array of white and slightly off-white shades to pick and choose from. From pure, dazzling 'art gallery' white to chalky, creamy or grey whites, there is the perfect shade out there for every style of interior.

pale and pure

The pureness of vintage china and old paper (above left and left) can provide inspiration for a white interior. There are myriad shades of white, from pure, clean white to softer, creamy whites. In places where the sun is strong (such as my home in the south of France), I prefer to use a white with a warmer tone, while in darker rooms filled with northern light (such as my Paris apartment), I go for a cleaner, purer shade of white.

add texture [overleaf]

An all-white scheme always needs the addition of texture and contrast to bring it to life. Warm wood and textiles, leather and fur all work well to soften up and bring a textural layer to an otherwise pure and plain room. Add small pops of black to add contrast and enliven the space (opposite and pages 82 and 83).

thundercloud greys

If I had to choose just one colour from the whole spectrum, it would be grey.
It may not be the most exciting colour, but it is certainly one of the most versatile.
Grey painted walls make almost any room look chic and pulled together, and they
provide the perfect backdrop for accent colours. In my own home, the bedroom is
painted a shade that is so dark that it is almost charcoal, and it has a very cosy,
cocooning effect. There are what feels like a million different shades of grey paint
available and they will look quite different depending on the light in your home.
I'm rather fussy – I don't like a grey that is too cold, but neither do I want one
that is too warm, so I always invest in a variety of tester pots and sample the
range before going all the way.

sink into grey

I tend to use a lot of grey textiles in my work
as a stylist, because they provide a great foil
for other colours. Grey linen bedding (below
left and opposite) is a particular favourite –
I think it's stylish, simple and inviting. You
can buy some excellent-quality linen sheets
in chain stores now, so they are a luxury
that's within everyone's reach.

Textiles are a good way to introduce colour to a room.
Bedlinen, curtains, cushions and throws will all allow you to
ring the changes without repainting the walls.

changing the backdrop

Painted backdrops are a brilliant way to add interest to
an interior, and they can be repainted at any time to ring the
changes. Here (this page and opposite), I used a few left-over
sample-size pots of white and grey paint and roughly brushed
them onto a large canvas rectangle. Once dry, I used it in my
spare bedroom to create the effect of a headboard. Don't aim
for perfection – I keep the brushstrokes deliberately loose and
uneven for a pleasing effect.

leafy green

Although grey is my favourite colour, green must come a close second. I find it has a soothing and calming effect, and it always makes me think of springtime. Due to my love of nature, green is an accent colour that I frequently use in my own home and when styling an interior. Whether it is a piece of furniture, a few branches of foliage, coloured glass or a bowl of vegetables, something green always seems to sneak its way in, as I think any composition needs a green accent to bring it to life. When it comes to decorating the home, there is a huge range of different shades to choose from, from silvery grey olive green to vibrant lime. Green can be quite overwhelming if you use it on all the walls in a room, so I would suggest tempering it with lots of white on the woodwork and floor to open the space up a bit and to make the overall effect less intense.

inspiration everywhere

Soft, smooth green is where my love of nature and my love of colour come together. I have to have living things in my space and I don't just mean flowers or houseplants – I often bring in a leafy branch or other foliage and display it like an artwork (opposite). When you are seeking colour inspiration, it can come from a variety of sources, including the velvety texture of ripe broad bean pods (above) and some vintage spools of green silk (above right) found on a market stall.

Soft, smooth green is a true inspiration from nature and it is an accent colour that I love to use both in my own home and when styling an interior.

green at home

Mix green with wood, white or natural colours to create an inviting interior. In the room shown opposite, large squares of sludgy green have been painted onto a white wall and framed by a band of cobalt blue to create interest and a sense of depth. Here (this page), a rich olive shade differentiates a simple wooden door from the planked wall surrounding it and creates a point of warmth and interest in a simple all-white room.

natural and neutral

I always prefer colours that are easy and enjoyable to live with, such as these natural neutral shades – they are soothing and cocooning, and work well with almost any accent colours. Natural hues, from pearly grey to earthy brown, always bring to my mind the summer months that I spend in the south of France. The earth is baked and bleached by the hot sun, muddy sand dries on the riverbanks, the fields are full of ripe wheat and small limestone farmhouses dot the landscape. Colour can be life-enhancing, yet so many of us struggle with choosing the right shades for our home. If you open your eyes to what's around you, you will find an amazing colour palette right under your nose.

Bleached beauty

When I was a child, I had a slight obsession with fossils and managed to collect quite a few over the years. Recently, I found some on a visit home to my parents' house and I still revel in their chalky texture and greyish-white hue (below left). Dried leaves (below) and soft linen bed sheets that have been washed dozens of times (opposite) share the same gentle, faded palette. I use these easy neutral hues a lot both in my own home and also when styling an interior.

When you feel like a change, a new rug, a couple of plump cushions or a soft, tactile throw can add just the right amount of colour to a room.

turning to gold

The rich golden brown shade of ripe wheat and dried goat's cheese (opposite and this page) reminds me of the long hot summers at my house in the south of France. It is a very soothing and comfortable colour to use on walls and furniture, and works well in both light and dark rooms, as it always looks soft and inviting.

soft earthy brown

Anything dried has always been strangely appealing to me. Dried leaves (this page), branches (opposite) and grasses all possess a mellow tone that reminds me of the soft darkness of the earth after a long day of rain. Even though it is quite sombre, I find this deep brown shade very soothing, and in the right environment it can look extremely elegant. I would use this colour on both walls and furniture. On the walls, it will create a room that feels very safe and cocooning, while furniture in this shade can look very stylish against a lighter-coloured backdrop.

bold contrasts

A little while ago, a friend asked what made this book different from my first book, *The Natural Home*. My answer was that I was working with much more colour this time around …like black. He looked confused – I think he expected me to say that the colour scheme was more bright and colourful! But to me black is a colour, and one that can add great contrast and interest to a white or light space. I love black kitchens, especially when dark cabinets are mixed with lots of white and wood. The effect is fresh and clean but less clinical than an all-white kitchen, which I find quite hard and stark. The secret to working with black is to add plenty of natural elements and textures, to soften the finished effect.

added depth

Darker colours, whether used as a backdrop or a feature, can create interesting effects. A black kitchen may sound intimidating, but if dark cabinets are combined with lots of white and wood, it will still look homely and inviting (left). You can easily soften up a black-and-white interior with plants and layers of different textures, which will create a more intimate and inviting feeling. In the home seen opposite, the owners made the brave decision to break up an all-white room by painting just part of the ceiling black. It's an unobtrusive way to add depth and interest to this corridor leading from one room to the other.

added details

When working with a graphic colour scheme, the little
details are so important. You can easily soften up hard lines
by introducing natural materials and vintage furniture (this
page). The black wall shown opposite is a real talking
point – the homeowners allowed the paint on the white
ceiling to drip down onto the matt black wall to create an
intriguing organic effect.

textiles

vintage pile

I have collected fabrics for as long as I can remember and have a hard time resisting buying more. Even though I am trying not to add to my collection, I still have to touch the beautiful fabrics that can be found at most flea markets. At home I have piles of mostly vintage, but some new, fabrics that I use, both in my work and to update the look at home. My collection includes neutral-coloured linen, faded floral prints and stripes, all made of natural fibres (opposite).

soft and safe

Felix, our whippet, also loves textiles. We always find him snuggled up on the sofa among the cushions, where he makes a cosy nest. I think it makes him feel comfortable and also safe, especially when we are not at home – and I think it is the same for us, too.

I have a passion for textiles and think they are a key ingredient in any home. We don't really consider how important they are to us and yet we use them every day, from drying ourselves after a shower, to sinking into the soft cushions of the sofa, covering up with a blanket on chilly evenings or curling up under the bed covers. We may take textiles for granted, but they are all around us, making us feel comfortable day and night and expressing our personality, just as the clothes we wear do. In the same way as we update our wardrobe from summer to winter, and add new pieces to keep on trend or to cheer ourselves up, textiles in the home can also be changed with the seasons, used to make a fashion statement or give a new injection of colour, whether in the shape of new cushions for the sofa, new towels in the bathroom or new sheets for the bed.

soft touch

I have a thing for linen napkins and use one at every meal (left). They are very easy to wash, so you can use them again and again. You can also simply pile them up on your kitchen counter to add a touch of softness to an otherwise hard space.

on a roll

I can hardly pass a roll of string without buying it, especially if it is made of linen (above). It is endlessly useful, but its wonderful texture and colour mean it can also just be a display piece.

relaxed look

This old folding camping bed made of weathered wood (opposite) was one of the first pieces I bought for our summer house in the south of France. I mostly use it inside as a place to read or snooze, layered with inviting cushions and throws.

linen and cotton

Natural-fibre fabrics are the only textiles I use within my own home. This is mainly because the more you wash them, the softer and more beautiful they become. I prefer vintage fabrics for this reason, as they already have the desired softness and patina. Vintage fabrics can be expensive to buy, but I think they are worth it for their wonderful tactility. They also seem to be stronger and of better quality than new fabrics. Even though they have been used for years, they can be washed over and over again and still look good. The secret behind this long-lasting quality could be that in the years before washing machines, fabric was always laundered very carefully by hand.

Both cotton and linen fabrics, whether old or new, come in many different weaves, structures and textures. I love to layer up textiles with looser and firmer weaves, and smooth and coarse textures. I also mix different shades of colour together to create multiple layers, especially neutral hues that are close to the colours you find in nature, but also dark tones contrasting with light. I nearly always use a linen cloth, runner and napkins when I set the table for breakfast, lunch or dinner, as it feels so much more festive than eating off a place mat or straight off the table. I think it is worth the extra washing because it makes everyday meals special – and every day should be celebrated, don't you think?

My home is a place for living, where you should be able to feel relaxed, happy and free, and the easy look of soft, wrinkled linen is so much more appealing than well-pressed fabric.

dressing for dinner

In both our flat in Paris and our summer house in the south of France, we dress the table for every meal. Eating at a dressed table gives the feeling of being in a restaurant, even though our tablecloths and napkins are not starched and pressed. Used table linen is simply thrown in the washing machine and then hung out to dry, ready to use again. I prefer fabric to have life and movement instead of being perfectly pressed, and linen looks so much better soft and wrinkled. I guess that is why I prefer it to other fabrics, as I am very lazy when it comes to ironing. The same goes for my clothes – the soft and wrinkled look makes me feel relaxed, which is also the effect I want at home.

plain and striped

I tend to use mostly plain-coloured fabrics in my home, but from time to time I mix it up with stripes or faded florals. I often sew cushion covers when I am on holiday, so there are always quite a few to choose from. I like the textural mix of these soft linen cushions with the vintage thick cotton ticking in smart blue-and-white stripes (right).

white cotton

Soft, slightly wrinkled cotton sheets make any bed look inviting (opposite). The knitted lace edging on these vintage sheets softens the white painted metal beds and gives the room a romantic feel. Cushions in different striped ticking add another layer of interest.

multiple layers [overleaf]

Beds made up with piles of cushions and layers of quilts and throws are the ultimate in relaxed comfort. I love to add extra cushions and throws to my bed, as it makes it feel so welcoming. I rarely use a bedspread, as I prefer to see the different textures and colours of my bedlinen. I also think it is important for the textiles to 'breathe' during the day. My bed in Paris (page 110) is dressed in soft, washed linen. I love the toning colours as well as the feel of the fabric – and it seems that our whippet Felix does, too.

My absolute favourite fabrics are French antique linen sheets. There is something about their texture – they are both coarse and soft at the same time – that simply can't be beaten. Over the years, I have amassed a fairly large collection of vintage sheets, as I know I will use and cherish them for a long time to come. They are so versatile that you can make nearly anything with them, such as cushion covers, curtains or a loose cover for an upholstered chair. I also sleep in either cotton or linen sheets, with a special love of linen, if I had to choose. The weight of linen sheets is very appealing to me and I find they make me sleep well. People tend to think that linen sheets have a coarse, rough texture, but I can assure you that they grow softer and more comfortable with every wash. There is nothing better, and with many great brands selling good-quality linen sheets at affordable prices, I would advise you to give them a try yourself.

without covers

Finding perfect vintage or antique upholstered furniture is not easy. Most of the time, the fabric is either tattered and torn or does not have the look or texture I am after. The shape, proportions and construction of these vintage French armchairs (opposite) are so pleasing, however, that I just stripped off the top layer of fabric and left them with only their original calico covers, revealing the wooden construction. Originally I had intended to have them reupholstered, but I fell in love with them stripped down to their bare forms, so simply covered the seats with large antique linen grain sacks to protect the fragile lining fabric (above).The simple daybed (left) has been given a new natural linen cover and, for extra comfort, large, soft pillows in washed natural linen and vintage French mattress ticking.

upholstery and cushions

When choosing sofas and armchairs, I tend to go more for traditional shapes than modern ones, as I prefer soft curves to clean, hard lines. I am often drawn to vintage upholstered pieces, both because of their shape and because they were made using only natural materials, including horsehair, hessian, cotton, linen and down. Most of the furniture dating from the seventeenth and eighteenth centuries was made to last with good-quality materials and workmanship, which makes it possible for us to use and cherish them even now. The fabric may need to be updated, which can be expensive, but the furniture will last even longer if you do this. The sofa in my flat in Paris is new, but the shape is classic and the loose cover is made from soft, natural-coloured linen that washes beautifully and will look better as it ages.

textile haven [overleaf]

If you love textiles, go all the way and create a soft fabric-filled corner to relax in. Here, even the walls have been draped with a heavy canvas fabric (pages 114–115). Simply nail it to the wall or, for a less permanent solution, use masking tape. Add large linen cushions for maximum comfort – these ones were made from antique linen grain sacks in soft, muted colours. The modern safari bed gives this corner a contemporary twist.

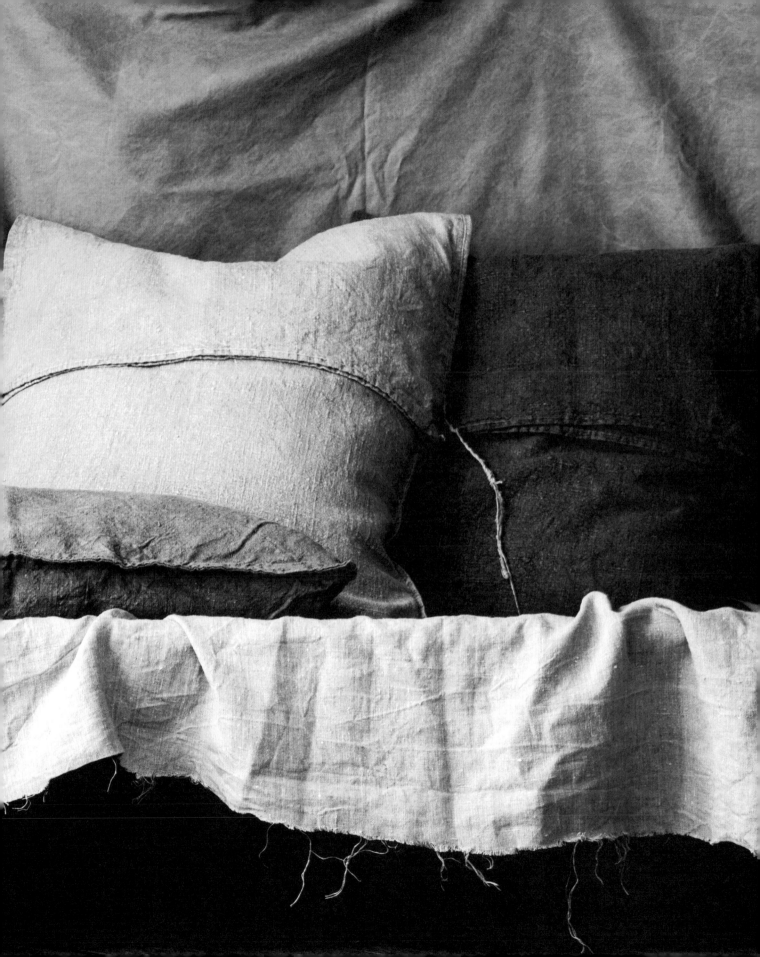

textural harmony

Using a mix of materials on your sofa gives an inviting and textural look. Linen, velvet and cotton in different weaves and textures all work very well together. For a harmonious effect, stick to colours from the same family, mixing soft pastels with darker and moodier hues to add layers and create interest. Introducing different-shaped cushions will make the arrangement softer and more lively than when using only the same shape.

vintage ticking [overleaf]

I can't have enough cushions and bolsters made from vintage Swedish striped ticking (pages 118 and 119), which I love for the quality of the fabric and the many variations of stripes and colours. These cushions are beautifully soft, as they are not too stuffed with down, so it is easy to create a relaxed and inviting look in any setting, whether simple and modern or textural and rough, as here. The blues of the fabric tie in with the rugged and uneven finish on the walls, and add softness and comfort to the space.

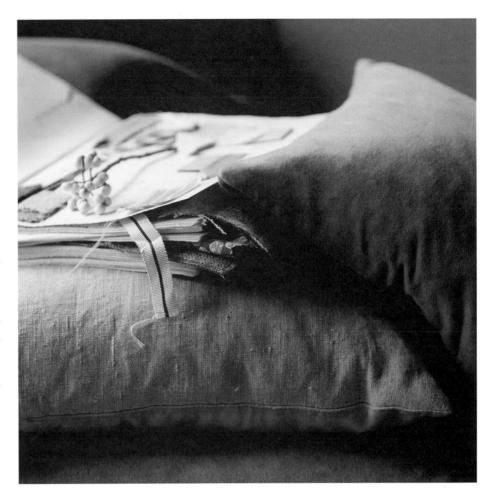

Textiles are the easiest way to change the look of a room in an instant, whether it's a simple colour injection or a seasonal shift from lighter, happier summer hues to a darker, moodier palette as winter closes in. A new cushion will give you that updated feeling, just like a new shirt.

I always choose down-filled cushions, for both the seating and scatter cushions. In addition to being more comfortable than foam-filled cushions, they are easier to work with when creating the soft, relaxed look that I find so much more inviting than something modern and strict. In my house in the south of France, for example, I have only armchairs and no sofa, which I think works really well for an informal room. Everyone gets their own seat, and the armchairs can be moved around much more easily than a heavy sofa to form different layouts and seating groups as the need or whim arises. I also change my cushions and throws on a fairly regular basis, as it is the easiest way to give your home a new look. Mostly I make them myself from my fabric collection, but once in a while I buy new, when I find colours that I can't resist.

backgrounds and drapes

Creating a textile backdrop is an easy way to introduce colour and pattern as an alternative to wallpaper or paint, and it instantly softens any space. You could use anything from a plain-coloured linen sheet or a faded floral print to a patchwork or embroidered piece that you have made yourself, and it is easy to change when you find a new favourite colour or print. You can also add throws or drapes to nearly anything in your home. I often use textiles on armchairs, sofas and tables to add texture and softness; it immediately makes an interior more welcoming. Historically, whole walls were often covered in fabric for insulation as well as decoration, and I am sure that layers of textiles – rugs on the floor, curtains at the windows and fabric on the walls – keep us warmer and happier.

hung up

The oversized wire hanger is the eye-catching piece in this still life of old wooden chairs and a painting cloth (left). The different materials and the muted colours mixed together create a textural focal point on any wall.

like a piece of art

A well-used painting cloth is something most people would throw away, but think twice in the future, as it can be used for so many things. Here (opposite), as a backdrop for a dining table, it almost looks like a piece of art. With its spatters of different colours and soft folds, it adds interest to the setting, which could otherwise look quite cold.

textural table [overleaf]

Drape cloth on your dining table to give it life and warmth. You don't have to use a perfectly ironed tablecloth – a tea/dish towel, a left-over scrap of fabric or, as here (page 122), a vintage piece of grain sack is enough to add that extra softness to your home, as is a pile of linen cushions on a stool or sofa (page 123).

homemade and painted

Since a very early age, I have loved making things with textiles. My mother taught me to use a sewing machine so that I could make my own clothes, especially when I had something special in mind that I couldn't find in the shops. They weren't the best-sewn pieces but it didn't really matter at that age.

These days, I don't make clothes, but I do sew a lot and find it very relaxing. Mostly, I make loose covers for vintage or worn armchairs, and cushion covers or patchwork using fabrics from the collection I have built up over the years. I never throw away any fabric, as even the smallest pieces can be used in patchwork or made into napkins or festive bunting to hang above a table. I especially enjoy piecing together patchwork quilts, as I find it very rewarding to mix and match different textures, colours and patterns to form something new and unique. Fabric is a great tool for dressing a room and adds softness to hard materials such as wood and metal. Whether in the form of curtains, upholstery or tablecloths, or smaller items such as bunting and cushions, the more tactile textiles you bring into your home, the more welcoming it will look.

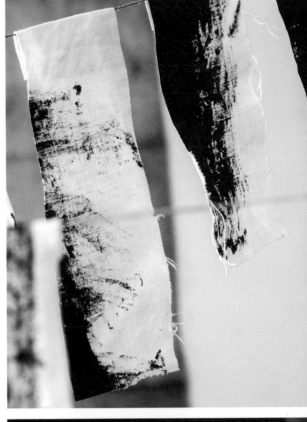

painted bunting

My latest craze is to paint on fabric, and any material seems to work well. I find textile paint quite hard to work with, so I use wall paint – most of the items I paint don't need to be washed, so it is safe to use. I paint larger pieces to use as backdrops – both for photoshoots and in my own home – and smaller pieces for bunting or other decorations. The bunting on these pages was made using left-over wall paint applied quite roughly onto a large sheet. I didn't want the paint to cover the fabric completely, as I wanted a textural look. When the paint had dried, I ripped the fabric into small pieces of different sizes and shapes and attached them to a length of string using double-sided tape. Using double-sided tape is the quickest way to make bunting and it holds really well.

textile cord [overleaf]

Now widely available, textile lighting cords are so much more attractive than standard black or white plastic ones, and it is not difficult to change them. If you don't have anywhere in your home to hang a pendant lamp from a textile cord, you can easily make a lamp by wiring up a simple light fitting and placing it in a large glass jar or vase (page 126).

handmade wall decoration [overleaf]

These antique cotton *zokin* cloths from Japan – layered pieces of old cotton fabric held together with *sashiko* stitching – have been used for centuries in homes, temples and schools to clean wooden floors and tatami mats. I found them in a flea market in Paris and it was love at first sight, not just because of the rich colours and textures, but also because of the history that these humble pieces of fabric have. I stitched them together to make this textural patchwork (page 127) and hung it on the bedroom wall, using a vintage rope to add yet another layer of textural interest to the display.

collections

no missing pieces

When I spotted this set of vintage rubber stamps at a flea market in Los Angeles (opposite), it was just too beautiful not to buy. The worn wood, the cut of the typeface and the fact that there were no missing pieces made my heart skip a beat – and, best of all, it was a real bargain.

flaking paint

I have a passion for vintage and worn paintbrushes (this page). I love their shape, and I also love the thought that someone has, with great effort and care, either painted houses, walls, windows and doors, or sat in front of an easel creating beautiful artworks.

I don't think of myself as a hoarder or even as a serious collector, but over the years I have managed to amass some very special pieces. As a child I always collected shells, pebbles, pieces of wood and forgotten treasures I discovered in my grandmother's attic. Today, I collect things that I fall in love with – old paintbrushes, vintage printers' blocks, vintage linen and anything else that catches my eye. And as a stylist and art director, I have the perfect excuse for buying new pieces because I need to update my (admittedly already rather large) collection of props – it's important to ring the changes every now and again, as every job has a different brief and story to tell. There are no rules on what a collection should consist of, but I think it is important to accumulate things that you will use and enjoy having around you. There is no need to rush the process – it takes time and effort to find the right pieces to add to a collection.

typography and letters

I have always been interested in typography – an interest that probably first developed while my father was working at a printing factory during my childhood. This was at the time when everything was laid out by hand, letter by letter and word by word. I can still remember the smell of the ink and how I loved to rummage through all the drawers filled with printing blocks and type in both wood and metal. I loved watching the printers slotting the letters together into a long line of text. It was such a precise and painstaking job. I expect I can't resist buying typography equipment now because it reminds me of that period of my childhood. It was a great pity that my father didn't salvage some of the letter blocks before the factory closed down, as they are truly small pieces of art. It gets harder and harder to find the genuine old ones, but as soon as I do, I bring them home, just to have them and admire the beauty of the craftsmanship and the type itself.

typography tableau

I have collected these vintage newspapers, advertising posters, old school counting sticks and wooden rulers purely for the style of their type and the beautiful colours they have turned with age (opposite). The French newspapers date from 1901. The way the typefaces have been used and the text laid out are so well considered, and the fact that it was all done by hand makes them even more beautiful to look at. I wish newspapers today would take inspiration from these masterpieces.

added value

I was so happy when I found these vintage 'good value' signs (above right). They made me realize how much care was once taken over the design of every sign — even for sales or promotions — and how ugly and badly designed today's equivalents are in comparison. It is as though we have forgotten that something designed to grab our attention can be made beautiful, instead of assaulting us with garish colours and unconsidered type.

labelled with love

I stumbled upon this old printed label at a flea market in New York City (right) and was immediately drawn to its faded, time-worn charm.

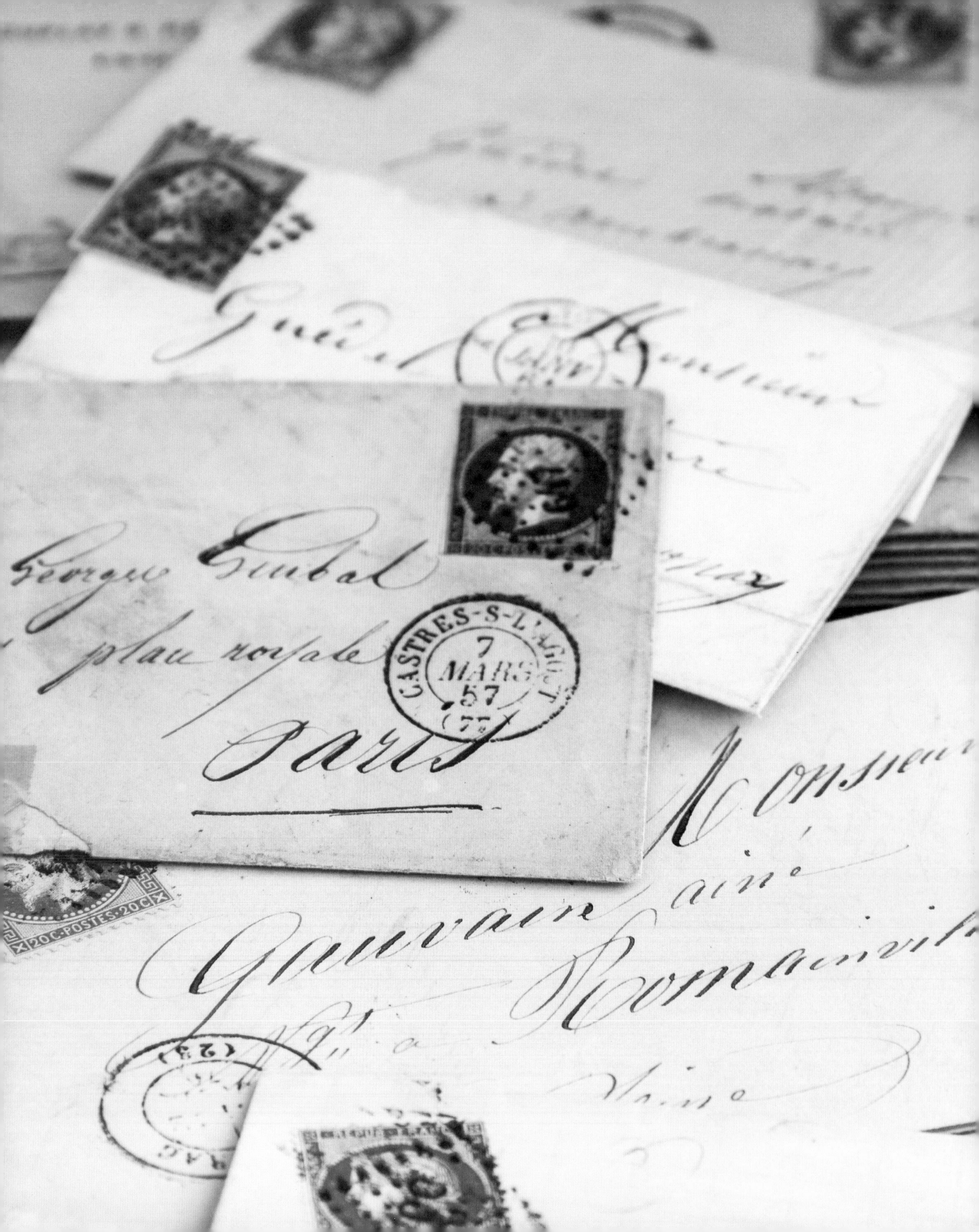
CASTRES-S-L'AGOUT
7
MARS
57
Paris
Monsieur
20C·POSTES·20C

handwritten art

The calligraphy on these French letters (opposite) is as beautiful as art. I wish I could read the Japanese postcards shown on this page. Surely they could tell a fascinating story – and I am intrigued to know how they ended up at a flea market in Paris.

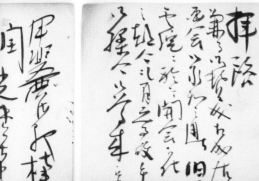

Photog

E. FRA

38

35

D60UB

ESCALIER D
CUISINES DE DROITE
& GAUCHE

COUR

CABINET
RUE des POISSONNIERS

PRUNIER Désiré F.
Cultivateur
à TILLY
Canton de Houdan (Seine et U

I collect vintage printed typography because I love all the different typefaces that were once used. In my view, a little of the beauty has been lost by today's methods – maybe because printing is done on a computer, not by hand, or because often too many different typefaces are used at once. Perhaps it is simply that working with typography used to be a true craft in which one specialized.

I also collect old letters and postcards, as the handwriting is always exquisite and one can see the effort and thought put into the writing of them. Today, as we write fewer and fewer letters by hand in favour of texting and emailing, I feel a need to collect handwritten letters because they will soon become a rarity.

just my type

I find it hard to resist old enamelled signs and letters, typewriter keys or anything with vintage type that comes my way (below left and right). They all come in useful when I want to add a graphic element to a picture for work or incorporate them into a display at home. Most of the enamelled signs (opposite) were found at a flea market in Paris. The USA is another fruitful hunting ground for good-quality typographic equipment.

I always keep my eyes wide open when I am at a flea market to see if I can find anything to add to my collections. Some of them have taken years to build up, as I choose only the very best pieces.

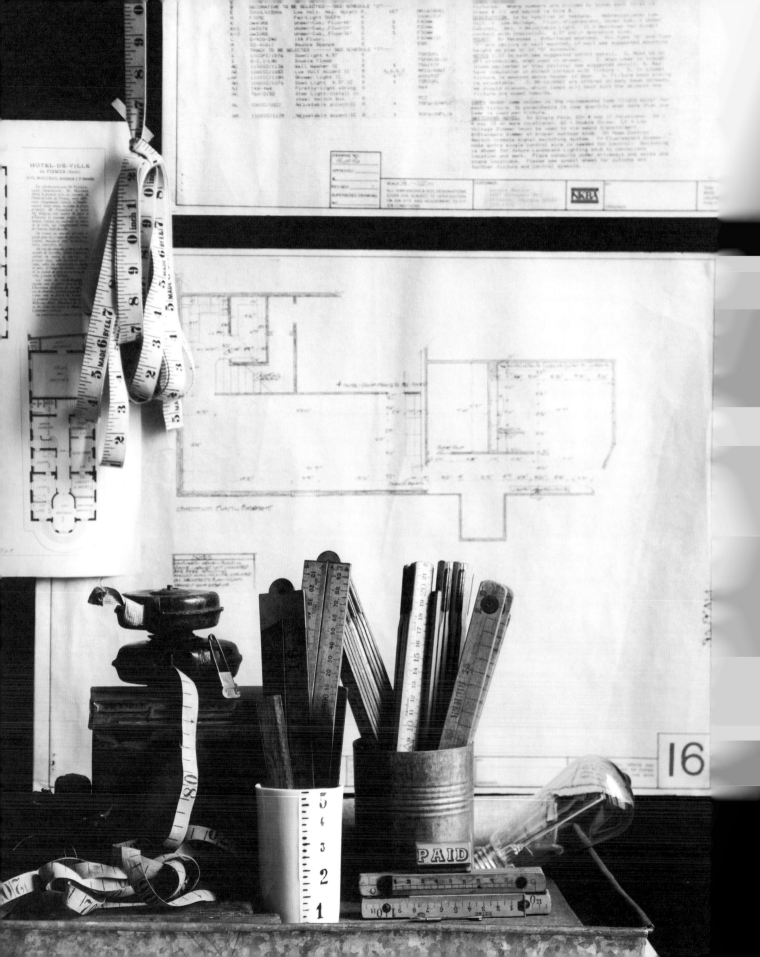

rulers and measuring tapes

One of the reasons I collect old rulers and measuring tapes is that they contain some of my favourite elements, such as well-worn wood and leather, softened through years of use and frequent handling, and, of course, beautiful typography. It is difficult to resist collecting an object that combines so many of the things I love in a single piece.

Most of my vintage rulers and measuring tapes were discovered at different flea markets around France and on trips further afield. I often use them at home to create different displays and still lifes, but I also take them to many of the photoshoots I work on because they add that little extra interest to a picture. I think it is important to introduce an element of textural contrast and add a couple of vintage pieces to any interior – even the most modern setting – as they always bring it an indefinable depth and charm.

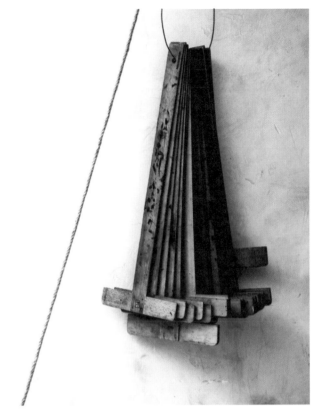

I collect things that I fall in love with – and that might be an old paintbrush, a piece of vintage typography, a glass vase or anything else that catches my eye.

on display

A collection of well-used wooden rulers and measuring tapes in leather cases sit well together in a simple yet eye-catching display (opposite). The vintage blueprints on the wall behind – found in a junk shop in Atlanta – make an appropriate background and tie the whole display together.

some favourites

This collection of wooden T-rulers (above right) came from a flea market in France. I bought only three to begin with but had to go back for the rest when I realized they would look so much better in a large bunch as part of a still life. I have a soft spot for these vintage measuring tapes in their leather cases (right). I love the shabby, time-worn leather alongside the graphic element of the fabric tape itself. As this type of measuring tape is now made from plastic, I just had to save some of the stunning examples from times past as a reminder that everyday objects can and should be both functional and beautiful.

simple china and glass

When it comes to china, I like to use a mix of vintage and modern. Items in everyday use tend to be modern, because they are less fragile and won't be damaged in the dishwasher. But I also use a lot of vintage china, as I love how it looks and feels, with a unique patina of age added through years of handling. I have a penchant for salad bowls – both small and large. Their appeal lies in their simple shape and the different shades of white that you find, depending on how much use they have seen. I always wash such pieces by hand, given that they have become quite fragile over the years. My china is mostly white – I think food looks so much more appetizing on white china. Another obsession of mine is vintage glass vases. You can never have too many, and although I can't say that I use them all, they are beautiful to display. I seek out only hand-blown glass vases, as their quality is far superior to those that are machine-made. The glass is always slightly uneven, so no piece is like any other.

pure white

My collection of china contains a bit of everything, even if most of it is kitchenware, both new and vintage. My favourite pieces are pudding bowls, shallow vintage salad bowls and simple spoons, all made in white porcelain (opposite). I also collect these beautiful small letters (above left), handmade at a little shop called Le Petit Atelier de Paris, which look stylish either on their own or added to a table setting with your guests' initials. The small dish (above), with the printed word *santé* ('health') at the bottom came from the same company in Paris. it is ideal to use at the table to hold nibbles or salt and pepper.

all clear

I have collected glass for a very long time and it is one thing I can't resist buying when I find it at a flea market. My favourite pieces are, of course, vintage, as I love the uneven quality and the slightly green tint of the glass. I either use these vases individually with a collection of objects, a simple bouquet of field flowers or a large branch, or I group them together so that their different shapes and heights create a beautiful display.

ribbons and thread

I have amassed a large collection of ribbons, ropes, strings and threads, since they are some of the most useful things to have to hand when working on a photoshoot or in my own home. Rope is so textural that it sits well in a bundle on a table or it can be used to hang lamps, baskets, large branches or even curtains. Ribbon is a great way to add colour, whether it is coiled in glass jars, used to hang decorations or tied around well-wrapped presents. I always try to find vintage pieces, as their quality and colours are more appealing. This is especially true of old rope, which has a characteristic worn and weathered look that can't be replicated. These humble accessories are a stylist's secret weapon. It is such a simple trick, but every time I add a piece of ribbon, a coil of rope or a spool of thread to a setting I have created, it instantly elevates the arrangement into something special.

beautiful and useful

I collect rope of any type, colour or texture – they are all different, but all very appealing to me (opposite). When it comes to ribbons, of course I always prefer vintage to new – even though I sometimes find it hard to cut them, especially when they are in their original packaging, which can be almost as beautiful as the ribbons themselves. In general, I have learned to be less precious about these things, as I think it is important to use whatever one buys and not keep it hidden away in a cabinet or drawer (below left and right).

There are a few things in life that I can never have too much of, and they include old textural rope and string, and vintage faded ribbons and threads.

brushes and palettes

Paint is one of my greatest passions. I started to draw and paint at a very early age and loved to experiment with oil paints. I can't claim to have produced any masterpieces – even though my parents have kept most of the paintings I produced at a young age – but it gave me the opportunity to play around with colour and texture. Nowadays, I find inspiration by visiting artists' studios and collecting anything to do with painting. Old paintbrushes and palettes encrusted with the colourful remains of oil paints are among my favourite objects to collect, as they seem to be imbued with the extraordinary creativity used to make art.

harmonious hues [previous spread]

I collect vintage wooden bobbins in any shape or form, with or without thread or string still wound around them, but these examples (pages 144 and 145) are among my favourites. Both the amazingly vibrant hues of the silk thread and the soft, muted colours of the yarn ones are very useful when I am looking for a specific colour reference.

artist's studio

It is easy to make a still life using old painting tools, as there is so much texture and colour to add different layers and interest to the display. Here, my collection of old brushes sits in clear glass vases so that they can be seen in their entirety, with their well-used bristles and the layers of paint on their handles (opposite and right). Large painting palettes hang from lengths of string on the wall behind, so both their shape and the built-up remains of paint that the artist has used can be seen to full effect. Vintage canvases propped up alongside complete the scene. A setting like this really makes me want to paint again. The scent of turpentine and oil paint instantly transports me back to my old bedroom at my parents' home where I painted as a child.

vintage collection

A stack of vintage French linen is truly beautiful (left and opposite). I think it is both the texture and the different shades of white that I find so appealing. When I started collecting linen sheets, it was possible to find them at bargain prices at flea markets in France, so I was lucky enough to gather quite a large number. I occasionally buy more, if I come across a new texture or shade of white that I just must have – it could become the perfect loose cover for a chair one day – but I definitely have sufficient for a few years of making ahead.

textural treasure trove [overleaf]

It is no secret that I love all the various textures of fabrics. The piles of pillows and fabrics shown here (pages 150 and 151) are a cornucopia of glorious textures in my favourite muted shades with the perfect vintage feel. All of these are either used every day on a bed or sofa, or are waiting to be made into something to add another layer of softness to my home.

It can be hard to find really beautiful antique fabrics today and unfortunately they are often quite expensive, but it is worth being patient and investing in pieces that are perfect for your home.

linen and other fabrics

Some things just get better and better through years of use, and one example is fabric, especially linen and cotton. I prefer vintage fabrics, as I love the softness from years of washing and the way the patterns and colours have faded. I have accumulated a large collection of fabrics over many years, and there is always a time and a place for them to take centre stage. My all-time favourites are antique French linen sheets, which can be used as tablecloths, curtains and throws as well as bed sheets, and can be made into anything from pillowcases and cushions to loose covers for chairs. If you don't want to keep them white, they are easy to dye different colours – ideally delicate, faded shades – without losing their unique vintage texture.

stencils and stamps

My interest in typefaces and graphic design is probably what first prompted me to start collecting stencils and rubber stamps. They are beautiful objects in their own right – and I often add them to a display or still life to great effect – but they also come in useful for decorating and personalizing all kinds of things. Stencils have been used for decades to make signs and I always photograph attractive old signs because they look so much more beautiful and characterful than their modern equivalents. My collection of stencils, most of which were found at various flea markets in France, includes ones made of both zinc and copper. Old rubber stamps are a great way to add a personal touch to letters or packages you are sending, or even just to mark your paid bills. Beauty is in the detail, and even the plainest of objects can become attractive when that extra effort is made.

personal touch

Stencils can be used in many different ways to add personal touches to your home. Instead of placecards on your dining table, simply tie the initials of your guest to their napkin. You can also print or paint words or poems onto a cushion or piece of fabric (remember to use textile paint so that it can be washed).

stamp it [overleaf]

When I buy vintage rubber stamps (pages 154 and 155), I always make sure they are still usable. I use them on letters and to label the cardboard boxes in which I store small props. Not only does this make it easier to find things, but it also makes the boxes more decorative to look at when they are displayed on a shelf.

Stencils and rubber stamps are both beautiful to look at and can be used over and over again. I always appreciate when that extra effort is made to make something just a little more personal.

Please Remit

NE PAS PLIER S.V.P.
ET PORTER A.U.B.

THINGS

STAMPS

STRING

THREAD

CARDS

ENAMEL

BAGS

L'AMPS

THINGS

RULERS

floral prints and flowers

In my own home, as well as in my work as a stylist, it is important for me to be able to create a variety of styles and looks – there are so many beautiful things around that I would never be able to go for just one anyway. As a result, my home is a mishmash of objects and furniture of different styles and from different eras. The neutral colour scheme makes the perfect backdrop for some things that are very old and others that are brand new, some that are patterned and others plain. The most creative spaces are fluid, whereas homes that are overstyled, where too much thought has gone into the process and where everything is matched to perfection, can feel strangely sterile and boring. Mixing styles, materials, furniture and other pieces from various eras makes a home so much more personal and interesting.

I have a real weakness for vintage floral prints, which fit perfectly into the neutral colour scheme of my home, adding another dimension and just a touch of colour and pattern.

french florals

When we are on holiday or in our house in the south of France, we always drink our morning coffee from these traditional French *café au lait* bowls (above left). These typical bowls with their distinctive floral prints were made in a town called Digoin in the 1930s by a company called Digoin Sarreguemines. The factories have now closed down, but you can still find these vintage bowls in flea markets all over France.

handmade treasure

I have a soft spot for anything handmade, and this quilt has been stitched and quilted by hand in the most precise way (left). The faded floral print features the most delightful shades of pink and duck egg blue and has been mixed so successfully with the blue-and-white striped ticking on the back. This was one of the first things I bought for our summer house. It was the perfect accent to add to the otherwise fairly neutral base that we used to decorate the house.

everlasting blooms

Also made and dyed by hand are these fragile but stunning fabric flowers (opposite). Fashioned from the most beautiful fabrics and with such exquisite detailing, they are perfect for styling romantic or decadent settings.

display

natural gathering

I love to bring plants and other natural items home with me. Here (opposite), I have suspended an armful of dried cow-parsley stems against a backdrop of vintage botanical prints that I found at a flea market. Seemingly unrelated, the different elements all come together in a display that adds visual interest and varying textures to a room.

hanging by a string

You can add displays to your home in many different ways – on a tabletop, sideboard, the walls or even the floor. Anything goes. One simple idea that I really like is to fix a length of string to a wall and attach smaller pieces that would get lost as part of a bigger display. Here, I have used miniature clothes pegs/pins, pieces of string and paperclips to secure my chosen objects (this page).

This chapter might give the impression that my home is full of beautiful displays and imaginative installations and that I am constantly tweaking and rearranging, but sadly that is not entirely true. I do have quite a few favourite pieces out on show, but my displays do not change quite as often as I would like. When you look at the same things everyday, the eye becomes so familiar with them that they just become part of the scenery. Also, as a stylist and art director, I spent a great deal of my time creating room sets and displays, so when I come home the last thing I want to do is create yet more arrangements. However, every so often I do make an effort to mix things up at home – it's so pleasing to the eye to see objects in different ways, and it's important to keep an interior fresh and updated. It seems to bring new energy to a space.

recycle and reuse

I always try my hardest to salvage, recycle and reuse things – to employ whatever I already
have to hand to create an arrangement that looks quite different, as well as finding a new use
for objects that have become obsolete. The cycle of fast fashion has reached the interiors
market and I think there is far too much unthinking throwing away in today's world. Instead
of slavishly following every new trend and rushing out to replace what we already own with
newer, shinier versions, we need to pause and re-examine our existing possessions. It can be
hard to break the cycle of constantly craving the new, but consider how you might be able to
give your things a new lease of life simply by showcasing them in a different context. The
world would be a better place if we all adopted the mantra 'rethink, reuse, recycle'.

fruitful

Vintage (or new) wooden fruit crates make
incredibly versatile storage receptacles. They
can be stacked up to create unusual modular
storage as well as providing a novel way to put
your treasures on display (opposite). The
weathered wood has a wonderful vintage feel
and brings texture to any kind of space. I use
fruit crates to hold magazines, table linen,
DVDs and even plants (right). They are also
useful in the kitchen as a temporary home for
newspapers and empty bottles for recycling.

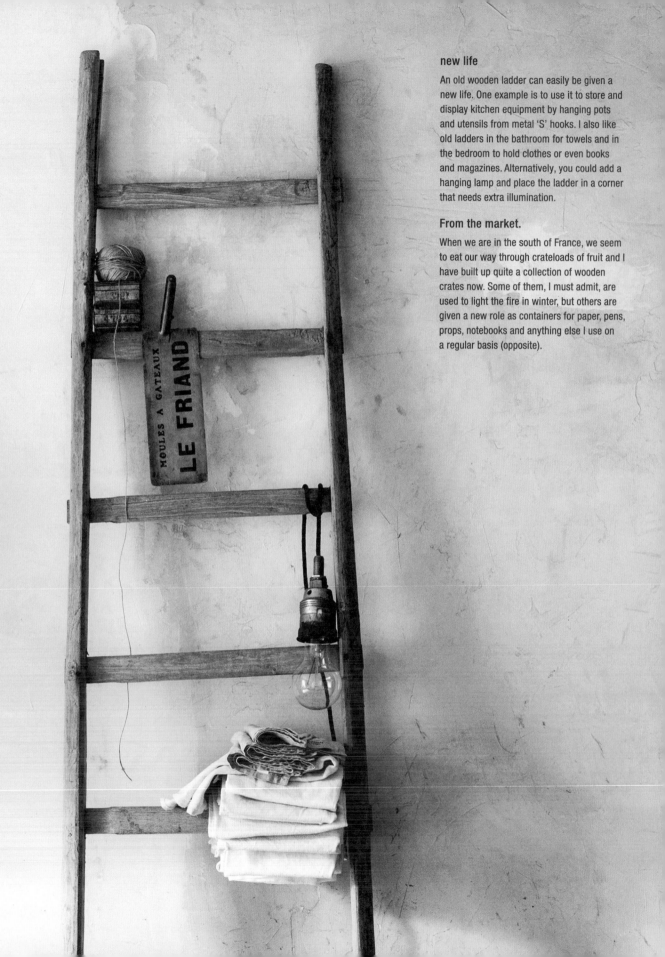

new life

An old wooden ladder can easily be given a new life. One example is to use it to store and display kitchen equipment by hanging pots and utensils from metal 'S' hooks. I also like old ladders in the bathroom for towels and in the bedroom to hold clothes or even books and magazines. Alternatively, you could add a hanging lamp and place the ladder in a corner that needs extra illumination.

From the market.

When we are in the south of France, we seem to eat our way through crateloads of fruit and I have built up quite a collection of wooden crates now. Some of them, I must admit, are used to light the fire in winter, but others are given a new role as containers for paper, pens, props, notebooks and anything else I use on a regular basis (opposite).

tabletops, shelves and other surfaces

Even as a very little boy, I loved 'stuff' and hoarded all the things I found – stones, branches, bird eggs or objects I found in my grandfather's studio, where nothing ever got thrown away. I carefully brought all these things (and more) home and added them to the collection of treasures that I arranged neatly on my bookcase and my desk – my first experiments with the art of display.

I am still a magpie today, constantly finding new things to add to my collections. The big question is, of course, where on earth to display all of my treasures? Displaying objects can be done in dozens of different ways and in almost as many different places, but perhaps the obvious starting point is flat surfaces – tables, shelves, cabinets and the like. We all have plenty of these

all propped up

A mantelpiece or even a narrow ledge can offer an opportunity for a simple display of smaller items (left). This collection of some of my favourite pieces of typography is propped along the edge of a piece of reclaimed wood. I have combined shiny gilt letters with vintage metal stencils, some of them suspended from a length of twine. The type theme is continued in the antique printing blocks and the sign on the wall. For a successful display, experiment with different textures and heights to interest the eye and create a pleasing composition. If you don't have any taller items, cheat by hanging something on the wall as close to the rest of the display as possible, and it will create the effect of height.

more than flowers

Over the years I have gathered a huge number of rolls of vintage wallpaper, old signs and posters, all of which are waiting to be framed or hung on the wall so they can enjoy their moment of glory. One day I realized that these objects could be stored and displayed in some of my glass vases (opposite). This way they are on constant display, rather than hidden away in a cupboard somewhere.

tone and texture

I love the mixture of shape, texture and height in this tabletop display. The very subtle, tonal colour scheme of brown and sludgy green means the arrangement requires contrasting textures in order to be effective. The glossy green leaves have a tactile leathery brown underside that is echoed in the papery husks of the dried corncobs below, while the sheen of the glass jars provides the perfect foil for the slightly wonky hand-turned wooden bowl.

surrounding us in the home, and you can group chosen objects on a table, along a mantelpiece, stacked on a chair or piled on the steps of a ladder.

Purely decorative displays are best situated on surfaces that aren't in everyday use – console tables, side tables, mantelpieces or wall shelves. To give a display some presence, it's best to find an element that provides a sense of height – a picture, poster or sign propped casually against the wall or hung just above the display works well, or you could also try a flag, a bust or even a large vase of fresh flowers or foliage.

If all the components of a display are roughly the same scale and height, the finished effect will be cluttered rather than composed, so think about mixing and matching different sizes, shapes and textures to interest and please the eye. If you look at the arrangements on these pages, you'll notice that I almost always add one item with a contrasting colour or texture – a reflective glass vase, gleaming metal or vivid green leaves.

Because I like my displays to look spontaneous and slightly random, I tend to opt for asymmetrical arrangements, but symmetry can create an equally pleasing if slightly more formal effect.

shades of grey

This very tonal display of items that share a moody neutral and grey colour scheme (opposite) is enlivened by the addition of a branch just coming into leaf.

a few of my favourite things

When you create a display, gather a few favourite things and start to play around. You don't have to run out and buy new items – anything can work. Here, an old book together with a vintage bottle provided the starting point for a display that also incorporates dried leaves and a spool of twine (above right).

printed on metal

This vintage *République Française* sign is one of my most recent finds (right). I think it is so beautiful, with its embossed lettering and rich colours. I have hung it from a vintage rope above a collection of vintage zinc pots.

hold it together [overleaf]

These two very different displays – one a collection of decorative objects, and the other consisting of more everyday items – have in common a deep blue background, which demonstrates how a dark backdrop can tie an assortment of disparate pieces together. On page 170, an arrangement of inspirational finds from different flea markets is dominated by branches of dried magnolia flowers simply arranged in a vintage glass jar. On page 171, a shelf made from an old piece of wood provides a home for neatly arranged books, old paintbrushes and various props left over from photoshoots.

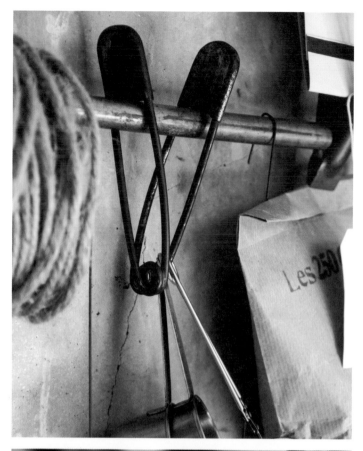

clip it

If at all possible, I prefer to avoid making permanent holes or marks on walls when I am creating a display. When showcasing two-dimensional objects such as posters, prints and cards, I use masking tape or adhesive putty to attach pieces to the wall, but to create three-dimensional displays I like to hang smaller items, such as vintage postcards, playing cards or letters, using clips or pegs. I often clip items to a length of string, rather like hanging clothes on a washing line, but there's no reason why you can't hang items from dried branches, as shown here. I find that onlookers can rarely resist taking a closer look at these intriguing arrangements!

Displays created using clips or pegs are easy to change, allowing you to ring the changes on a regular basis and with minimal effort. Over the years, I have amassed a large selection of clips in different forms, material and sizes and I always snap them up when I spot them (particularly vintage examples), as they are always sure to come in useful. On the following pages there are a variety of ideas that you can steal for your own home – I hope you will find some of them inspiring.

clip it on

One of the best ideas that came to me when I was gathering ideas for this book was using the large dried branch shown here (opposite and below left) as a sort of three-dimensional noticeboard. Using mini bulldog clips, I attached a selection of cards, colour swatches and letters and realized that this was a decorative display solution for a desk or hallway – you can attach an assortment of bills, notes and letters and you won't forget them.

jumbo pins

I stumbled across these large safety pins (above left) in a flea market in Williamsburg, New York City, and I just couldn't resist them. They work brilliantly on a rail in a kitchen to hold a bunch of drying herbs or various utensils.

nature's bounty

In my summer house, I suspended some dried flowers and leaves from a length of twine using vintage clothes pegs/pins. The graphic poster was a later addition to bring a contemporary edge to the arrangement. The great thing about using clips or pegs to create displays is that you can add and subtract items as the fancy takes you.

clip it up

I am not a fan of framing vintage or old prints as I find it hard to find modern frames that suit them. Paperclips, bulldog clips or clothes pegs/pins are perfect for displaying prints or posters, as you can use small tacks to attach a clip to the wall, then just hook on your picture – it makes for a very casual and spontaneous effect (opposite).

hanging around

In a small guest bedroom, there isn't always enough space to squeeze in a wardrobe or closet. A length of twine is a perfect solution for temporary clothes storage and looks striking too (this page). The coathangers are a mixture of vintage and homemade.

walls

When it comes to display, I think we underestimate the potential of walls. Yes, we display pictures, posters and mirrors on them, but there are so many other possibilities. You can hang small pieces of furniture on a wall, put favourite pieces of clothing out on display, suspend bags, hats, vases and other small objects from hooks and even dangle pieces from cord or rope (which, by the way, is also a brilliant way of adding texture to an arrangement).

Arranging and displaying artwork is a subject that really deserves a whole book to itself. Perhaps it is the easiest and least challenging type of display, as we are all familiar with the notion that pictures should hang on walls. But people often get worried about whether pictures and posters are 'good enough' or 'important enough' to be put on permanent display, and it can be nerve-racking hammering nails into a pristine wall, as it feels as if there's no going back.

I like to be able to change and alter displays
whenever the mood takes me so I use adhesive putty,
masking tape or washi tape to attach pictures,
posters, maps or cards to my walls.

quick change

The easiest way to display your favourite prints and cards is by using adhesive putty, commonly known as Blu-Tack or Poster Putty. This brilliant invention doesn't damage paintwork and makes it easy to change and rearrange wall displays (opposite). I do like to move things around and try out new arrangements, and this is the best solution I have come up with so far.

wonderwall

Clear your floor and table space by hanging things on the walls. I attached this chair to the wall using a short length of rope and a screw (below). It now serves as a shelf to display a few chosen objects. A simple glass vase also makes an effective three-dimensional wall display (below left). All you need is a rimmed vase, some string and a nail.

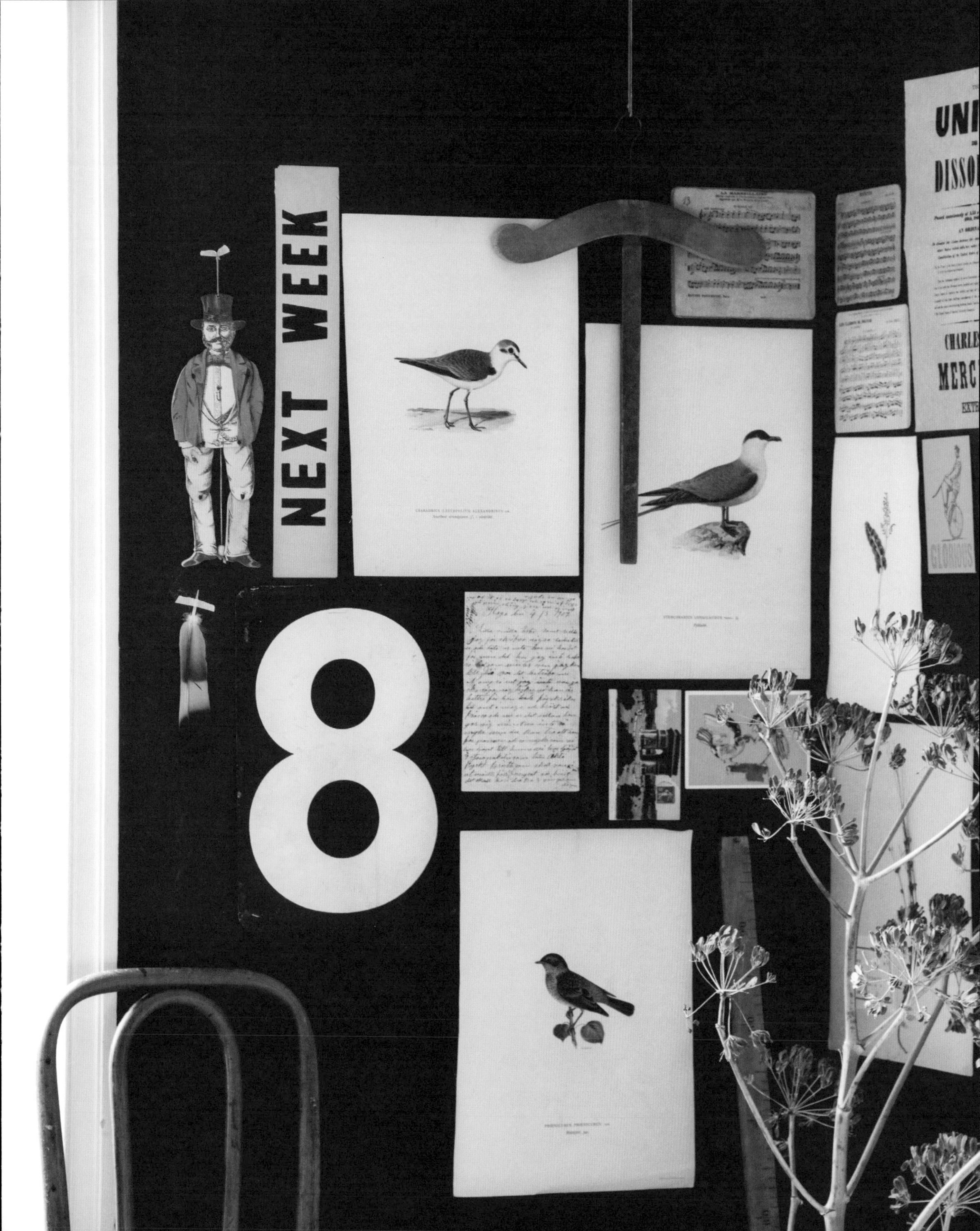
NEXT WEEK
8
GLORIOUS

materials and texture

Displaying sketches, bags, labels, pictures or tear sheets can easily be done without covering the walls with tape or adhesive putty if you use either a square of metal grille (this page) or an old wire tray (opposite). This makes it easy to just simply tie or clip on anything that takes your fancy. It's a good way to display family photos, labels, sketches or anything else you want to keep close to hand without damaging your wall.

A RHYTHM BETWEEN
SPACE, ARCHITECTURE
& SCULPTURES
LIKE THE IRREGULAR
FLOWING IDIOM OF THE
BAROQUE ERA

LE LABO®
GRASSE — NEW YORK

Personally, I like to be able to change and alter displays whenever the mood takes me, so I tend to use either adhesive putty, masking tape or Japanese washi tape to attach pictures, posters, maps and cards to my walls. If you like to change things around frequently, another good solution is a giant pinboard or a metal grille, as shown on the previous spread. Use pins, bulldog clips or pegs to hold things in place, and you can swap things around whenever the mood takes you.

Art gallery walls are usually pure white and it's true that a plain, unobtrusive backdrop ensures that whatever is on the walls draws the eye, rather than the wall itself. But I also think that dark walls frame some objects beautifully, especially black-and-white photographs, old posters and bold type.

Walls aren't just the natural home for artworks. You can also create displays with plants, flowers, textiles, tools, household implements and even lights. As long as an item can be safely secured and doesn't create an obstacle, it can be displayed on the wall.

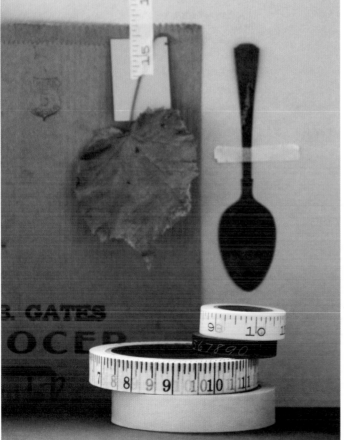

fallen leaves

I love it when the seasons change and autumn comes creeping in, even though I have a slight sadness that summer is over. Since a very young age, at this time of year I collect fallen leaves and press them between the pages of a heavy book. I decided to make an autumnal display by taping the dried leaves to a wall, where their rich colours and varied shapes can be marvelled at. The easiest thing to use for a display like this is masking tape or washi tape, as it does not leave any marks when you peel it off the wall (left and opposite).

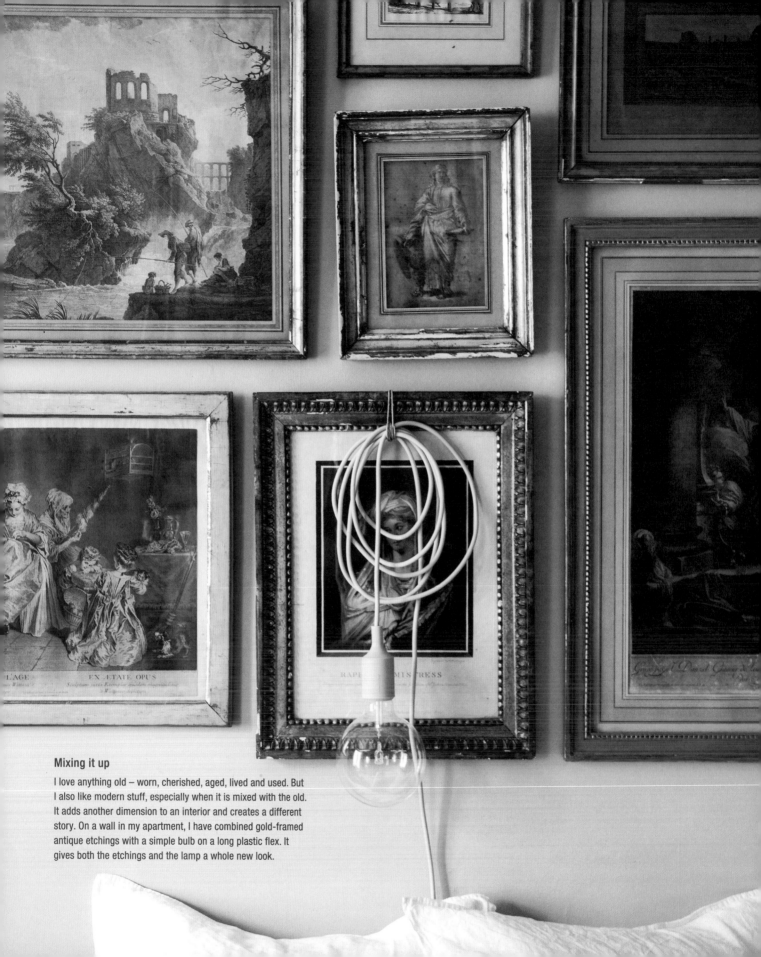

Mixing it up

I love anything old – worn, cherished, aged, lived and used. But I also like modern stuff, especially when it is mixed with the old. It adds another dimension to an interior and creates a different story. On a wall in my apartment, I have combined gold-framed antique etchings with a simple bulb on a long plastic flex. It gives both the etchings and the lamp a whole new look.

Anything goes

When it comes to displaying the things we love, anything is possible. A favourite piece of clothing or other accessories – hats, jewellery, shoes – can easily be part of a display. This jacket is one of my favourites so it enjoys a special place in my home. Something about its shape, colour and structure appeals to my eye, and it will age beautifully. I think it will be part of a display for a long time... or at least until the next favourite comes along!

pleasingly practical

There are certain areas of the home, such as bathrooms and kitchens, that have a practical role to play, but I think it's important that they have a personal touch as well. Of course, a kitchen is a functional area that requires adequate space for food storage, preparation and cooking, and it needs to be planned with care, as an efficient layout and enough storage will make everyday tasks – cooking, emptying the dishwasher – so much easier. However, I firmly believe that even the most utilitarian items – stacks of pots and pans, or piles of cutlery/flatware, for example – can be shown off in an aesthetically pleasing fashion. This is where display crosses over into storage and starts to play a practical as well as a decorative role.

As you can probably tell, I am not a fan of minimalist interiors and I do like to have all my things around me whether I am relaxing, working or cooking.

kitchen inspirations

Add personality to your kitchen by hanging posters and labels with a culinary theme (opposite). These posters are designed and produced by a Swedish company called DRY Things owned by my friends Jenny and Johan.

stamp it out

I used luggage labels and rubber stamps to make these hand-printed labels and tied them to my kitchen storage jars (below left).

softly, softly

A stack of washed linen napkins add welcome texture to a kitchen's hard surfaces (below).

YOUR BUTCHER VARIOUS PRIMAL CUTS

#1 CHUCK	#4 RUMP	#7 FLANK
#2 RIB	#5 ROUND	#8 PLATE
#3 LOIN	#6 SHANK	#9 BRISKET

CHUCK Pot Roast Stew Smothered Steak Ground Beef Cross Rib | **RIB** Rib Roast Rib Steaks Rib Eye Roast or Steak | **SHORT LOIN** T-bone Porterhouse Club Steak Tenderloin Strip Steaks | **SIRLOIN** Sirloin Steaks Top Sirloin Tenderloin Tri-Tip | **RUMP** Pot Roast Stew Smothered Steak Ground Beef | **ROUND** Strips & Cubes Pot Roast Stew Jerky Smothered Steak Chicken Fried Steak Ground Beef Oven Roast Oyster Steak | **SHANK** Chili Ground Beef | **FLANK** Flank Steak Jerky Strips for Stir-Fry | **PLATE** Ground Beef Short Ribs Stew Skirt Steak | **BRISKET** Pot Roast Stew Corned Beef Barbecue.

THE KITCHEN GARDEN

HERBS

Italian Kitchen	French Kitchen	Asian Kitchen
BASIL	TARRAGON	CORIANDER
OREGANO	CHERVIL	LEMON GRASS
SAGE	THYME	SWEET BASIL
ROSEMARY	MARJORAM	SPEARMINT
PARSLEY	FENNEL	LEMON VERBENA

A CUP OF TEA
Chamomile, Peppermint, Spearmint

SAGE

ROSEMARY

Les 250 g

In a kitchen, instead of fitted cupboards, I prefer open shelf units, which are the perfect home for items that form an attractive display in their own right, such as baskets, vintage china or exotic foodstuffs. Shelves also help to keep the work surfaces free of clutter. I much prefer them to fixed wall cabinets, which I find bulky and intrusive. Instead, look for quirky vintage cabinets to hang on your wall. Alternatively, you could stack up fruit crates, hang shelves or fix simple rails to the wall so you can hang up the things you use everyday.

If you are lucky enough to have a lot of storage space, you will be able to devote your walls to decorative displays. Opt for kitchen themed pieces – tear sheets of recipes, vintage menus, or posters with a culinary theme.

close to hand [previous spread]

In a kitchen, items in frequent use should be kept close to hand. I like to hang all sorts of things on my kitchen walls, either suspended from a simple metal rail that I have screwed straight into the wall (page 189), or dangling from lengths of twine. In the south of France, we harvest and dry many different herbs – they are not only deliciously tasty, but also beautiful to look at. I stumbled across the old zinc labels in a flea market in Paris – they would have been used to label wine in a winery long ago (page 188).

out on show

I think open shelving in kitchens is really beautiful – it adds visual variety and interest to a working environment (opposite). If I ever have a new kitchen, I would definitely choose something similar to this sleek unit – I love the stacked plates and bowls, which create a layered yet orderly effect. You could add washed linen 'curtains' as door fronts to introduce some texture or keep the shelves dust free. Vintage chopping boards provide a great contrast to gleaming stainless steel kitchen appliances (left).

outside in

In Paris we are not lucky enough to have any sort of outside space, but this didn't deter me from creating a garden-themed still life. I gathered together a few vintage garden objects, including a lovely old metal watering can and some sacking, then brought the composition to life by adding bulbs and seedlings in terracotta pots and sticking a few pages from an old portfolio of botanical prints to the wall.

still lifes

Don't be daunted by the concept of creating still lifes. The most important thing to remember is that they absolutely do not have to be perfect – just personal. Arrangements such as these should first and foremost be a collection of objects that you love – old vases, vintage ribbons, porcelain objects, seashells, flowers, woodworking instruments.

In the same way, there is no right or wrong when it comes to creating the composition – it's entirely up to you. That might sound quite intimidating, but you have all the time in the world to play around with the various components.

behind glass

If treasured items are precious or fragile, placing them beneath a glass cloche will offer a measure of protection (right) and discourage viewers from touching them. The wall behind the cloche has been 'wallpapered' with vintage architect's drawings that I bought in a junk shop in Atlanta.

tone on tone

For displays with a very harmonious, serene quality, opt for items that share the same colour scheme but possess contrasting textures and shapes to create interest. Here, my collection of Japanese postcards (see page 133) are combined with a dried eucalyptus branch and a tangle of vintage rope. This is one of my favourite displays.

beautiful baskets

I bought these large Chinese baskets in the south of France (opposite). I loved their shapes, texture and colours at first glance, and they are so versatile that they make a perfect addition to almost any display. I use them for storing rolled-up posters, long brushes and my collection of ropes.

Whether at home or at work, putting together displays is
something I love to do. I can spend hours arranging
different objects to create a harmonious whole

a moody backdrop

It's easy to create temporary backdrops for a display. Here (opposite), I attached large sheets of handmade paper to the wall using adhesive putty. The dark indigo, nearly black shade is moody and intriguing and provides the perfect foil for the pink berries attached to the almost bare boughs.

on the road

I don't know why, but this still life makes me think of a road trip (right). It has a sort of freewheeling, spontaneous feeling to it. The vintage brown medicine bottle was found at a flea market and made the perfect holder for wild branches studded with red berries.

If something isn't working you can just shuffle everything round, adding a couple of items or subtracting a couple of others. When you feel happy with the arrangement and it pleases your eye, then you'll know you've got it right.

I see many displays and still lifes featured in magazines and interiors books which give the impression that for a successful still life you have to invest in dozens of new designer items that share a colour scheme or a common theme. That's not the way I do it. For me, anything goes, and sometimes it's the most unlikely objects that come together to create the most successful displays. One of the best things is giving my treasures a new lease of life by showcasing them in different ways and matching them up with new favourites. Have fun, play around and enjoy the creative process of putting together a display.

old friends [overleaf]

Wood is one of my favourite materials, thanks to the rich patina it develops as it ages (page 199). Here, it plays the starring role in a carefully composed display (page 198). All the items included in this arrangement have been part of my collection for many years. Faithful old friends, they have appeared in a multitude of different settings in my own home as well as travelling with me to many photoshoots.

address book

My personal selection of shops all over the world.

LONDON

Camden Passage Market
Islington
London N1 5ED
*Lively antiques market
with small stalls selling
vintage clothing, jewellery,
collectables and homewares.*

Labour and Wait
85 Redchurch Street
London E2 7DJ
+44 (0)20 7729 6253
www.labourandwait.co.uk.
*Vintage-inspired hardware,
including old-fashioned
enamelled kitchenware and
simple utilitarian glassware.*

Leila's Shop
15–17 Calvert Avenue
London E2 7JP
+44 (0)20 7729 9789
*A shop and café situated next
door to each other. The shop
sells both food and kitchen
hardware and a few books.
The café serves amazing
brunches!*

Josephine Ryan Antiques
17 Langton Street
London SW10 0JL
+44 (0)20 7352 5618
www.josephineryan.co.uk
*Antique furniture, textiles
and mirrors, all carefully
selected by Josephine.*

SWEDEN

A La Carte Antik
Riddargatan 11A
114 51 Stockholm
+46 (0)8 661 99 88
www.alacarteantik.com
*Antique and vintage
porcelain, tableware and
glassware. Also some
furniture and collectables.*

Brandstationen
Krukmakargatan 22
118 51 Stockholm
+46 (0)8 658 30 10
www.herrjudit.se
*Great selection of vintage
home accessories and
fashion pieces.*

Dusty Deco
Kocksgatan 23
116 24 Stockholm
or at
Horntullsrand 7
117 39 Stockholm
+46 (0)70 315 66 36.
*One of the best shops in
Sweden – a great mixture
of vintage furniture and
accessories.*

DRY Things
Upplandsgatan 36
113 28 Stockholm
+46 (0)8 218 800
www.drythings.se
*Gorgeous graphic and
photographic posters
(some featured in this book),
leather bags and soaps.*

Evensen Antik
Upplandsgatan 48
113 28 Stockholm
+46 (0)70 346 21 30
*One of my favourite antiques
shops in Stockholm – a great
mixture of finer antiques but
also interesting junk. I always
find something here.*

GAMLA LAMPOR
Sibyllegatan 18
114 42 Stockholm
+46 (0)8 611 90 35
www.gamla-lampor.se
*Specialists in antique
and vintage lamps as well
as antique watches and
furniture.*

Garbo Interiors
Brahegatan 21
114 37 Stockholm
+46 (0)8 661 60 08
www.garbointeriors.com
*Another favourite of mine.
An inviting home design
shop with a great selection
of antique and vintage
furniture mostly from
France and Sweden. Also
some interesting new
designs plus plants.*

Paper Cut
Krukmakargatan 24-26
118 51 Stockholm
www.papercutshop.se
*The best magazine shop
in Sweden, where you will
find almost any magazine
available. They also stock
back issues. An absolute
must for magazine lovers!*

FRANCE

L'Arrosoir
102 rue Saint-Maur
75011 Paris
+33 (0)1 43 57 15 61
*My favourite flower shop in
Paris. The selection of flowers
and plants is always amazing
and the shop looks like a
mixture between a flower
shop and a junk shop.*

Atelier 154
16 rue Neuve Popincourt
75011 Paris
+33 (0)6 62 32 79 06
www.atelier154.com
*Specializes in industrial
vintage furniture plus smaller
items and decorative objects.*

Caravane
6 rue Pavée
75004 Paris
+33 (0)1 44 61 04 20
www.caravane.fr .
*Luxurious sofas, beds and
lighting, but also an amazing
textile collection with
curtains, rugs and fabric
sold by the metre.*

Merci
111 boulevard Beaumarchais
75003 Paris
+33 (0)1 42 77 00 33
www.merci-merci.com
*Concept store with both
homewares and clothing.
Great selection of linen
sheets and kitchen textiles.*

L'Objet qui Parle
86 rue des Martyrs
75018 Paris
+33 (0)6 09 67 05 30
My all-time favourite shop in Paris. Packed with interesting vintage bits and pieces, I could (and do) spend hours browsing here.

Marché Paul Bert/Serpette
96–110 rue des Rosiers/
18 rue Paul Bert
93400 Saint Ouen
+33 (0)1 40 11 54 14
www.paulbert-serpette.com
Open Saturdays through to Monday. Market offering mostly French antique furniture and objects.

Le Marché aux Puces de Vanves
Avenue Georges Lafenestre
75014 Paris
+33 (0)6 86 89 99 96
Open Saturday and Sunday mornings between 7am–1pm. Well worth getting up early for, as I always find great and interesting objects here.

Le Petit Atelier de Paris
31 Rue de Montmorency
75003 PARIS
+33 1 44 54 91 40
A boutique-atelier of two young designers. The shop hosts fine hand-made china objects for everyday use and display with a graphic touch.

USA

ABC Carpet and Home
888 & 881 Broadway
New York, NY 10003
+1 212 473 3000.
www.abchome.com

One of my all-time favourites, so very inspirational. Brilliantly edited products including the latest modern pieces of furniture and amazing vintage pieces, alongside jewellery and household products.

The City Foundry
365 Atlantic Avenue
Brooklyn, NY 11217
+1 718 923 1786
www.thecityfoundry.com
Stacks of mostly industrial antiques, with everything from furniture to lamps to smaller objects.

Big Daddy's Antiques
3334 La Cienega Place
Los Angeles, CA 90016
+1 310 7696600
www.bdantiques.com
An amazing, eclectic collection of antiques, vintage pieces and junk.

Greenhouse and Company
387 Atlantic Avenue
Brooklyn, NY 11217
+1 718-422 8631
www.greenhouseandcompany.
com
Antique and vintage furniture – everything from storage to tables and chairs. Also new sofas and smaller items, both vintage and new.

Hell's Kitchen Flea Market
112 W 25th Street
New York, NY 10003
+1 212 243 5343
www.hellskitchenfleamarket.
com
Open Saturdays and Sundays all year around. I think this antiques garage is my absolute favourite flea

market. I always find so many interesting things here, mostly smaller objects, clothes and junk but also some pieces of furnitures. A few blocks down is another open-air flea market.

John Derian Company Inc.
6 East Second Street between
2nd Avenue and the Bowery
New York, NY 10003
+1 212 677 3917
www.johnderian.com
Three stores next to each other on the same street, selling handmade découpage with reproduced imagery from their studio in New York. There's also furniture, both newly made and antique, and smaller objects both vintage and new. One of my favourite New York shops.

Paula Rubenstein
21 Bond Street
New York, NY 10012
+1 212 966 8954
Antique and vintage furniture and a great selection of interesting and unique objects both for collecting and displaying. Also a great range of vintage fabrics and quilts. Always worth a visit.

Williamsburg Flea Market
50 Kent Avenue (between
N.11 and 12 St)
Brooklyn, NY 11211
+1 718 928 6603
Open Sundays only. A great selection of vintage and antique objects and furniture. Some clothes and fun junk pieces too.

WRK Design
32 Prince Street
New York, NY 10012
+1 212 947 2281
Industrial furniture and lamps, with lots of small things, ideal both for collecting and displays.

COPENHAGEN

Leif Sigersen
Lille Strandstraede 15
1254 Copenhagen K
+45 25 56 61 37
www.leifsigersen.com
Jewellery and seasonal decorations made from both vintage and modern materials.

NO 40
Gammel Kongevej 39A
1610 Copenhagen
+45 31 98 18 62
www.no40.dk
An eclectic array of French vintage and industrial furniture, with everything from large farmhouse tables to metal filing cabinets, chairs and stools. Also a large selection of vintage objects including lamps, baskets and other lovely decorative pieces.

Fil de Fer Store
Kongensgade 83A
1264 Copenhagen
+45 33 32 32 46
www.fildefer.dk
A haven for anyone with a passion for French antiques and objects. Lars, the owner, has gathered a beautiful and interesting collection in his shop. Well worth a visit.

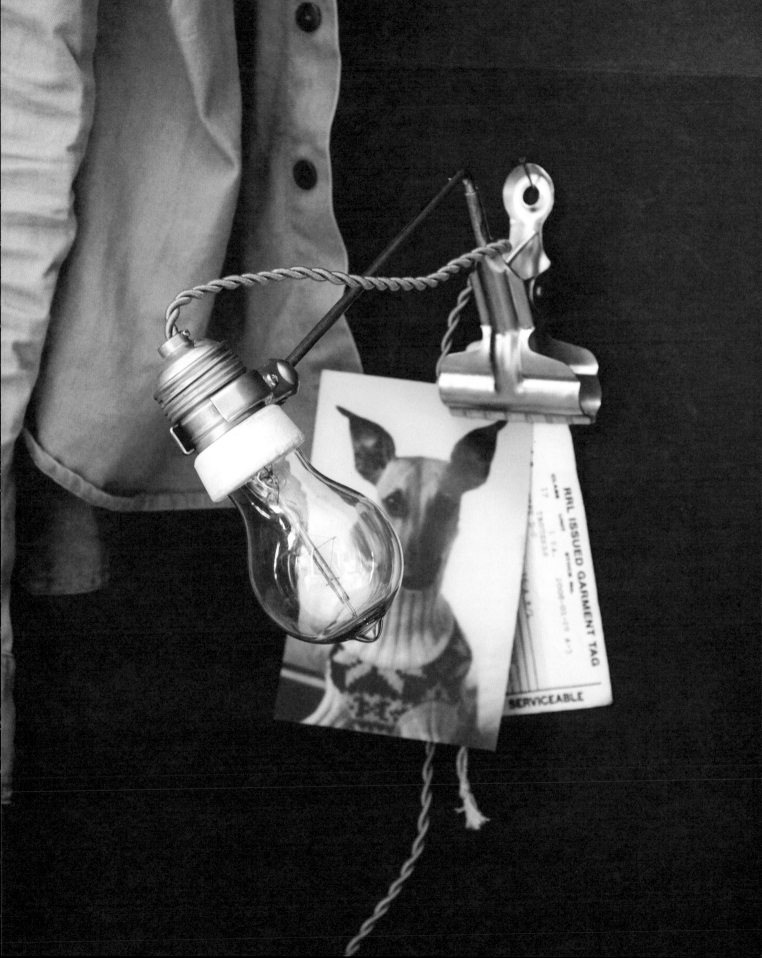

picture credits

All photography by Hans Blomquist except the following which are by Debi Treloar:

1 The home of film director Christina Höglund in Österlen, Sweden; **13 right** Next Door's space Brooklyn, to rent for events and photo shoots www.nextdoorsp.com; **34–35** The home of film director Christina Höglund in Österlen, Sweden; **38** Home of writer and director Tannaz Hazemi; **39** Next Door's space Brooklyn, to rent for events and photo shoots www.nextdoorsp.com; **42** Next Door's space Brooklyn, to rent for events and photo shoots www.nextdoorsp.com; **44–47** Next Door's space Brooklyn, to rent for events and photo shoots www.nextdoorsp.com; **50** The family home of Harriet Maxwell Macdonald of Ochre.net in New York; **52–53** Kvarngården. The home of photographer Nils Odier, stylist Sofia Odier and their two daughters Lou and Uma. Skivarp, Sweden; **58–59** Next Door's space Brooklyn, to rent for events and photo shoots www.nextdoorsp.com; **60** Home of writer and director Tannaz Hazemi; **61 above** Home of writer and director Tannaz Hazemi; **61 below** The home of film director Christina Höglund in Österlen, Sweden; **62–63** The home of film director Christina Höglund in Österlen, Sweden; **64** Home of writer and director Tannaz Hazemi; **65** The home of film director Christina Höglund in Österlen, Sweden; **70–71** Next Door's space Brooklyn, to rent for events and photo shoots www.nextdoorsp.com; **72–73** Home of writer and director Tannaz Hazemi; **76** Next Door's space Brooklyn, to rent for events and photo shoots www.nextdoorsp.com; **78** The family home of Harriet Maxwell Macdonald of Ochre.net in New York; **81, 83, 84 left** and **85** Kvarngården. The home of photographer Nils Odier, stylist Sofia Odier and their two daughters Lou and Uma. Skivarp, Sweden; **88** Home of writer and director Tannaz Hazemi; **90–91** The home of film director Christina Höglund in Österlen, Sweden; **98–101** Kvarngården. The home of photographer Nils Odier, stylist Sofia Odier and their two daughters Lou and Uma. Skivarp, Sweden; **109** The home of film director Christina Höglund in Österlen, Sweden; **111** The family home of Harriet Maxwell Macdonald of Ochre.net in New York; **116–117** The family home of Harriet Maxwell Macdonald of Ochre.net in New York; **118–119** The home of film director Christina Höglund in Österlen, Sweden; **120–122** Next Door's space Brooklyn, to rent for events and photo shoots www.nextdoorsp.com; **166–167** Next Door's space Brooklyn, to rent for events and photo shoots www.nextdoorsp.com; **180** Kvarngården. The home of photographer Nils Odier, stylist Sofia Odier and their two daughters Lou and Uma. Skivarp, Sweden; **191** The family home of Harriet Maxwell Macdonald of Ochre.net in New York; **202** The home of film director Christina Höglund in Österlen, Sweden.

business credits

Christina Höglund
House available for rent
T: + 46 73 531 29 21
E: lama@telia.com
Pages 1, 34–35, 61 below, 62–63, 65, 90–91, 109, 118–119, 202.

Next Door's Photo Studio
67 34th Street
5th Floor, Unit 11
Brooklyn, NY 11232
T: + 1 917 544 1559
E: Francesco@nextdoorsp.com
www.nextdoorsp.com

and

Carin Scheve
Styling – Art Direction
T: + 1 917 587 3883
www.carinscheve.com
Pages 13 right, 39, 42, 44–47, 58–59, 70–71, 76, 120–122, 166–167.

Tannaz Hazemi
E: tannaz_hazemi@yahoo.com
Pages 38, 60, 61 above, 64, 72–73, 88.

Ochre
London Head Office & Showroom
46–47 Britton Street
London, EC1M 5UJ
T: + 44 (0)20 7096 7372
E: enquiries@ochre.net

and

New York – Downtown
462 Broome Street (between Mercer and Greene)
New York, NY 10013
T: + 1 212 414 4332
E: usenquiries@ochre.us
Pages 50, 78, 111, 116–117, 191.

Sofia Odier
www.agentbauer.com
52–53, 81, 83, 84 left, 85, 98–101, 180.

index

thank you!

Debi, it is always such a true pleasure to work and to hang out with you. Thank you for saying yes to this project, even though I decided to shoot half of it myself. You are one of a kind – a dear friend, a true star and so amazingly talented.

Frederick and Felix, thank you for coping with me turning our homes upside down and making them into temporary photo studios. And thank you for everything you do for me every single day.

Annabel, Leslie, Jess, Cindy, Toni and Lauren at Ryland, Peters and Small, thank you for letting me do another book. It is such a great pleasure working with you all...you are amazing.

I am so grateful to all the people who let us shoot in their homes, and took such good care of us while we were there. It was such a pleasure to be able to visit different homes and feature them in this book, and without this kindness, the pages would not be easy to fill.

Thank you to my parents, who let me explore my creativity in my own way while growing up and who still support me in every possible way and cheer me on. Thank you also for letting us stay with you for weeks on end when working in Sweden, and for taking such good care of us and, especially, Felix.

Thank you to Nicole Watts for helping me out in NYC and for being a good friend. And thank you to my Instagram friend @haruyomorita, for helping me identify the Japanese handwriting on pages 133 and 194.

Thanks to everyone who bought my first book, *The Natural Home*. Without your support, there might not have been a second book. I hope you find *In Detail* equally inspiring and full of ideas that will encourage you to make your home your very own special place. Thanks are also due to my clients all around the world, for giving me the opportunity to work with you and to develop and grow your company's style and communication. Without you I would not be who I am today.

And to everyone who buys this book...it is intended to give you lots of inspiration so I do hope you enjoy it. Thank you! For more details, follow me on Instagram @hansblomquist.